Miles Glendinning is head of the Topographical and Threatened Buildings Surveys at the Royal Commission on the Ancient and Historical Monuments of Scotland. Aonghus MacKechnie is Principal Inspector of Historic Buildings at Historic Scotland. Both contributed to *A History of Scottish Architecture from the Renaissance to the Present Day* (1996), and Miles Glendinning is also the author, with David Page, of *Clone City: Crisis and Renewal in Contemporary Scottish Architecture* (1999).

Thames & Hudson world of art

This famous series provides the widest available range of illustrated books on art in all its aspects.

If you would like to receive a complete list of titles in print please write to:

THAMES & HUDSON
181A High Holborn
London WC1V 7QX

In the United States please write to:

THAMES & HUDSON INC.
500 Fifth Avenue
New York, New York 10110

Printed in Singapore

Miles Glendinning
Aonghus MacKechnie

Scottish Architecture

195 illustrations, 68 in color

Thames & Hudson world of art

Foreword and Acknowledgments

This book contains a short history of Scottish architecture from the beginnings of continuous human settlement to the present day – a period of about ten thousand years. The story is arranged chronologically, in six chapters. We aim to give a concise overview account of each period, outlining the main architectural trends in their wider cultural and social context, and identifying the most important individual works. The book is concerned both with architecture in Scotland and, to a somewhat lesser extent, architecture by Scots elsewhere: given the small size of the country, ambitious designers have often sought their fortune beyond its frontiers, especially during the years of British imperial power. Inevitably, too, with Scotland's deep involvement in the modern world movements of empire, industry, and urbanization, the narrative is weighted towards more recent centuries, especially towards the supremely diverse and creative 19th century. At the end, a brief conclusion considers whether any common themes or strands arise out of the story as a whole.

We would like to thank our families for their support during the writing of this book, and also to acknowledge the help or advice given by the following: Patrick Ashmore, Malcolm Bangor-Jones, Gordon Barclay, David Breeze, Shirley Brook, Michael Burgoyne, Ian Campbell, Alison Darragh, Stephen Driscoll, Richard Emerson, Richard Fawcett, Ian Fisher, Sally Foster, Emily Lane, Rod McCullagh, Aidan and Lorna Matthew, Stefan Muthesius, Geoffrey Stell, Margaret Stewart, Susanna Wade-Martins, and Diane Watters.

First published in paperback in the United States of America in 2004 by Thames & Hudson Inc., 500 Fifth Avenue, New York, New York 10110

thamesandhudsonusa.com

Library of Congress Catalog Card Number 2003101351
ISBN 0-500-20374-1

Designed by John Morgan
Printed and bound in Singapore by C. S. Graphics

(title page)
1 Victorian eclecticism in the suburban landscape: Woodlands Hill, Glasgow, seen with Kelvingrove Park in the background. In the foreground are classical terraces of the 1830s and 1840s by George Smith. The towers of Free Church College (by Charles Wilson, 1856–61) and Park Church (by J. T. Rochead, 1856–57) are in the centre of the view, and behind is Park Circus, ringed by Park Terrace and Quadrant (all by Wilson, begun in 1855).

Contents

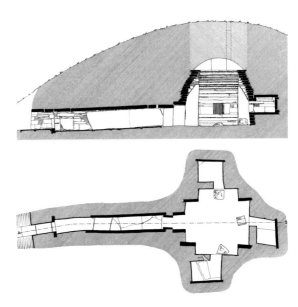

2, 3 Maes Howe, Orkney,
c. 3000 BC: interior of the
rectangular main chamber (above),
and section and plan, showing the
entrance passage, and main and
side chambers.

Chapter I   Prehistoric and Early Historic Scotland

4000 BC to AD 500:
Monuments of Earth, Stone and Sky

Tombs and Early Houses: the Neolithic and Bronze Ages
The early hunter-gatherers of the Mesolithic period constructed
only the most ephemeral buildings, and their tent-like homes
have left almost no trace. With the appearance of farming in the
Neolithic period, from around 4000 BC, came a greater need
and capacity to begin shaping a 'built environment'. With few
exceptions, houses remained flimsy: the main effort was devoted
to creating communal monuments for ritual use within the wider
landscape, linking agriculture to seasonal and celestial patterns.
In the early Neolithic period, there was no attempt to
'monumentalize' everyday life: it was the timeless realities of
ancestor worship that seemingly dominated people's religious
beliefs, and the principal built structures were collective tombs.
Later in the Neolithic Age, there was a move towards centralized
power, represented by elaborate circular ritual sites governed
by astronomical orientations: the focus of worship shifted from
the earth to the sky.

Although it would be a fallacy to claim direct continuity
between the Neolithic and later ages, perhaps some of the ancient
locational decisions, even at several removes, helped shape the
landscape of today's Scotland. A fundamental regional division
emerged, between the northern and western seaboard and
islands, and the southern and eastern mainland. Monumental
stone structures predominated in the former, and more
ephemeral timber and wood in the latter – a difference that has
radically skewed today's archaeological record.

During the early Neolithic years, massive chambered tombs
or cairns were built in hundreds or even thousands across the
country for about one and a half millennia [2, 3]. These formed part
of a wider European tradition of passage-graves, and constitute
Scotland's first permanent architectural constructs –

a wonder of the prehistoric world, built several hundred years before the Egyptian pyramids. They contain one burial chamber or more, sometimes reached through a stone-lined passage, and often corbel-roofed in stone and topped by a cairn of stone boulders or earth. But it is misleading to see chambered cairns solely or chiefly as burial places. They may have served mainly as more general places of ritual assembly – in other words, as temples – with most people being buried elsewhere. Two broad regional formulae are discernible: in the south and east, earth-covered long or round barrows are prevalent, whereas in the north and west stone construction is dominant, with tomb walling of flat-faced boulders pinned upright, roofs of corbelled layers of stones, and non-structural portal stones marking entrances and divisions.

With its shortage of trees and its excellent building stone, including readily available flagstone slabs, Orkney has some of the richest and most finely constructed survivals, densely clustered in places, and falling into two broad categories. First, there is the 'stalled' type, as at Isbister, c. 3000 BC, with a rectangular chamber with byre-like partitions on each side. Second, there are tombs with central chambers entered from passages. The exemplar of this pattern is Maes Howe [2, 3], also c. 3000 BC, comprising a square main chamber and lesser side rooms; a sloping entrance passage permits the midwinter sunset to shine on the back wall of the main chamber, possibly allowing ceremonies connected with cosmology and the seasons. As well as élite rituals within the tombs, more general outdoor assembly is implied by the splayed wing-walls or 'horns' flanking the entrances of some tombs. The only two large enclosed Neolithic places of assembly so far excavated in Scotland (and Britain) are hall buildings of c. 3600 BC at Balbridie in Aberdeenshire and Claish in Stirlingshire, built of outer and inner perimeter rows of upright timbers, and with many internal supports.

Very few houses of this early period survive, and then almost exclusively in the stone-building areas of the north and west, especially in Orkney. The oldest stone-built houses in north-west Europe are at Knap of Howar (3500–3100 BC). This farmstead contains two near-parallel, thick-walled, roughly rectangular 'houses' standing directly up against each other – a plan-form which continued in Orkney and Shetland farms up to the 19th century. The walls, partitions and benches are of stone slabs. The best-preserved of a sequence of settlements in the Northern Isles is the group at Skara Brae [4], c. 3100–2500 BC. Houses here are

4 Skara Brae, Orkney: the winding passageway between the dwelling-huts of the settlement, c. 3100–2500 BC.

part-subterranean, with stone walls packed around with middens, and slab partitions and roofs; rooms have central hearths, inset wall-recesses, and basins sunk in the floor, and there are also tiny rooms with drains (possibly latrines). The hearths are mostly oriented as at Maes Howe, dictated by the sunrise and sunset at each solstice. The unity of design and orientation indicates a community for whom cosmological influence was powerful, and shared by both living and dead. Defensible structures on islets, related to the later crannogs (see below), developed very early in the Outer Isles, where many lochs have natural, often causewayed islets, as at the Neolithic site at Eilean Domhnuill, North Uist, c. 3000 BC. In the Bronze Age, from around 2000–1500 BC onwards, the roundhouse formula, popular throughout Britain and Ireland, began to take hold.

The greatest energy was put not into architecture but into communal, ritual monuments. The largest, mostly constructed during the years 3600–3100 BC, are the 'cursus monuments' –

5 Calanais, Lewis: aerial view of the religious site, 2900–2600 BC. In the centre is the circular 'henge', surrounding a single monolith; from it lines of monoliths radiate in a cruciform pattern.

enormously elongated rectilinear enclosures up to 2 kilometres (1¼ miles) long, flanked by ditches or embankments: the only visible example today of these vast landscape interventions is the Cleaven Dyke, by Meikleour, Perthshire (c. 3300 BC). From about 3000 BC, many individual temples or religious sites were laid out, defined by great avenues and rings of large stones (megaliths) or timber blocks, commonly laid out in a circular 'henge' pattern. One of the earliest datable stone circles is Stenness, near Maes Howe, with which it is roughly contemporary; in the same vicinity is the Ring of Brodgar. The three sites may all have been ritually linked. Calanais, in Lewis (2900–2600 BC) [5], has a uniquely complex form, with a central monolith ringed by a stone circle and an outer cruciform pattern of radials. In the Bronze Age, around 2000 BC, the 'Clava' group of monuments around Inverness and Nairn combined stone circles with circular burial cairns, originally with corbelled stone roofs and some containing a single burial. From around 2000 BC onwards, all these types of collective monuments and temples were gradually phased out, and greater emphasis was put on buildings for the living, such as houses and forts.

Homes for the Living: the Iron Age
From around 700 BC, the number and variety of surviving archaeological remains increase sharply. The introduction of iron prompted a radical restructuring of existing trading routes, and, possibly, a growth in local autonomy. There was a new awareness of locality, territory and the 'home', but, until the early centuries AD, little evidence of overarching political organization. These

trends were apparently reflected in a proliferation of high-status structures for everyday life, such as enclosed and defensible buildings in groups ranging from a handful to hundreds of houses.

Circular plan-forms became dominant, and although tombs were no longer built, their technology lived on in the drystone walling, stone-lintelled passages and boulder mounds. The roundhouse formula diversified and reached monumental proportions in the form of tall stone towers, while promontory

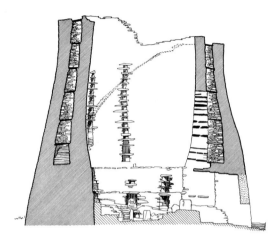

6 Mousa Broch, Shetland, c. 200 BC–AD 100: section. Intermittent bonding stones in the hollow walling create internal air-circulation galleries. Two scarcement ledges at the bottom (shown as lines of stones) possibly supported upper floors, and a stair (the curving line) led to the top.

7 Mousa Broch in its landscape setting.

and hilltop sites saw an explosion of fortified structures known as duns. All seem variants of a common tradition. The primary distinction between the stone-building Atlantic north and west and the non-stone south and east continued, but the roundhouse pattern was common to both. Symbolic or actual defence became a greater concern, and settlements might be surrounded by stockades. The household structure of these settlements, and the degree of collective living or definition of the individual dwelling, is not clear.

In the Atlantic zone, a distinctive architectural tradition of habitation emerged in the first millennium BC, focused on massive drystone roundhouses, mostly with conical thatched roofs. Present-day surviving traces are of substantial buildings with complex internal divisions, in various forms known as brochs, crannogs and wheel-houses. Duns overlap with the roundhouse type, although the largest were essentially small forts containing entire communities. The cultural significance of large roundhouses is uncertain. The more extensive, nucleated examples, such as Gurness in Orkney, imply a hierarchical culture with élites and servants; but some of the larger structures on the Atlantic seaboard may have been occupied in a semi-collective, multi-household manner.

The dominant Iron Age dwelling-type of the north and west, built in some numbers from around 200 BC to AD 100, was the broch: a frequently tall, monumental, windowless circular block profiled like a modern cooling tower. The broch was drystone-built and double-walled, with intramural spaces and one or more staircases. Its interior was a great tapering shell, probably roofed overall, and possibly with one or two upper floors. Doorways and passages were low and flat-headed, often with triangular lintels. In the far west, brochs were usually freestanding, sometimes (as at Dun Bharabhat and Loch an Duin, Lewis) occupying islets, like crannogs. Typically, the entrance faced away from the line of easy approach. The best-preserved broch, at Mousa in Shetland [6, 7], survives to a height of over 13 metres (45 feet), and has a central space only 5 metres (16½ feet) across. The hollow walls of this monumental structure contained three ground-floor cells and five galleries above, reached by a continuous staircase. In some places, as at Gurness, the broch was the centrepiece of a settlement of smaller cellular dwellings and other structures for everyday use, within a ditched outer perimeter. The towers within these 'broch villages' may have been intended partly as redoubts during sieges, with livestock kept at ground level. Overall, the purpose of brochs and the reasons for their design are still debated – in particular, as with early medieval castles, whether their massive form was mainly a practical, defensive feature, or mainly symbolic, rendering them as showpieces of a highly stratified society and its powerful leadership.

Another, linked strand of the roundhouse tradition of the late Bronze Age/Iron Age and early historic period is the crannog, of which many hundreds were built – a massive dwelling-block surrounded by water, usually by being set near the shore of an inland loch, river or estuary on an islet either intentionally modified or even built from new. Access was by log-boat or by a stone or timber causeway, which might continue as a platform around the house. Some sites were re-used and rebuilt continuously right up to the onset of the Improvement movement in the 18th century.

Crannogs consisted of large timber superstructures, resting on substructures that follow two general patterns, though without a hard-and-fast division. In the north and west, solid foundations made it possible to have platforms composed of hundreds of tons of boulders; elsewhere, especially in the south-west, thick mud required pile-supported rafts or platform mounds of peat, timber and brushwood. A range of uses for the structures has been posited, all involving mixed or communal functions: they might have served as protection for livestock or the harvest, as cargo landing-places, or as defensible dwellings. Proximity to arable land seems to have been important. Like brochs, crannogs were immensely technically challenging and labour-intensive in relation to the accommodation they provided.

In strong contrast to these somewhat extravagantly engineered, extrovert buildings, in the last few centuries BC the roundhouse tradition in the exposed north-west and Shetland took an introverted direction, digging down instead of building up. Interestingly, the areas where these 'wheel-houses' were prevalent almost never coincide with the areas where brochs were built with accompanying settlements. These circular, sunken structures, exemplified by Jarlshof, Shetland [8], typically consist of a round pit dug in coastal sand and given a stone-lined interior with an inner perimeter of piers (the 'spokes'), lintelled and corbelled, creating simultaneously a base for medial roof supports, a perimeter of cells, and a massive wall-head at ground level. Over it all was a timber-framed conical roof; the wall-head was capped by clay or turf.

The pattern of domestic building is rather different in the east, centre and south of Scotland. Here too there was wide regional and individual variation: settlements, for instance, might be unenclosed or they might be sheltered within a palisade. However, a hierarchy not seen in the Atlantic zone is implied by massive hillforts and duns such as Traprain Law in East Lothian [9], which seem to have served as regional centres. Duns and brochs were stone-built, while houses were usually of earth and timber. Houses of the late Bronze Age/early Iron Age tended to be massive, as for example the 'ring-ditch' houses of Tayside and East Lothian – indicative perhaps of multiple functions within. A house at Scotstarvit in Fife which may date from this period was 19 metres (some 62 feet) in diameter; it had a large entrance hall and three concentric rings of posts, all within a circular enclosure. By the late 1st century BC, houses in the south-east tended to be considerably smaller.

In the south-east and south-west, hillforts and enclosed settlements abound. They range widely in area and in the scale of their ramparts. Some contained only a few dwellings, while others, such as the south-eastern regional centre of Eildon Hill North in the Borders, contained an extensive mixture of houses, ranging in date from the late Bronze Age to the early 1st millennium AD. It is not clear how enclosed and unenclosed settlements differed functionally: perhaps enclosure was a regional custom rather than a necessity.

The isolated hill of Traprain Law [9] is probably the most prominent Iron Age hilltop site of all. There is no decisive archaeological backing for the claims that it was either a key trading centre during Roman times or the 'capital' of the Votadini (the 1st-century AD Roman name for the relatively pacific south-eastern tribe): some evidence hints at a hiatus in occupation of several centuries prior to the Roman age. Yet major ritual deposits do suggest it was extremely important, possibly as a communal and ceremonial centre for the farming settlements all around.

Pointers to the Future: Roman Interventions in Scotland
On three occasions between the 1st and 3rd centuries AD, Rome mounted major invasions and partial occupations of Scotland, with the intention of completing the conquest of the present-day island of Britain. The first, during the Flavian dynasty, lasted from c. AD 70 to 88; the second was in 140–65 during the reign of Antoninus Pius; and the third was in 208–11, under Septimius Severus, who led one campaign in person. None of these was successfully consolidated, but each left its own built legacy, sometimes superimposed on its predecessors, as in the camps at Ardoch, Perthshire.

As there was no permanent colonization and Scotland remained a frontier zone, the direct legacy of Rome consists largely of military remains, some of empire-wide significance. These are naturally concentrated in the areas of campaign and temporary annexation, in southern Scotland and especially in Perthshire/Angus, a borderland territory of prime agricultural value. No villas, towns, elaborate public buildings or mosaic decoration are known, although there were a few extra-mural civilian settlements such as Inveresk in Midlothian. The physical remains are supplemented by the first (very limited) historical documents concerning Scotland, including inscription slabs and written accounts. We also encounter the first named 'designer' known in Scotland, a military engineer called Amandus (perhaps a freedman), who set up a religious statuette at the camp of Birrens, Dumfriesshire, in 210. In addition to these direct interventions, there are also more elusive traces of the impact of Rome on local Iron Age settlement and agriculture.

During the first stages of the Flavian invasion, led probably by governor Quintus Petillius Cerealis in the early 70s, the Romans initially advanced as far as the Highland line, building the 'Gask Frontier', an array of six forts or fortlets and eighteen watchtowers dotted at intervals along a military road linking the Forth and the Tay – the very first of the many artificial barrier-lines in the Roman Empire. During the later consolidation phase, which included Agricola's well-known campaign in AD 82, a further, outer line of forts was built from the Clyde to Stracathro in Angus, blocking the exits from major glens, as well as some forts on the Forth–Clyde line. In addition, more isolated forts were built to support attacks into the Highlands, including the grandest of all: Inchtuthil [10], a legionary fortress located near Dunkeld, Perthshire, in a uniquely strategic position on the north bank of the Tay, at the junction of the main routes to the north and the north-east.

The invaders imposed their own building forms, stereotyped throughout the empire. In general this was architectural design in its most simplified and (in the case of marching camps) ephemeral form. Yet we should bear in mind that throughout the extremities of the empire, the rigid grid layout and standard components of these camps and forts were the first experience of planned settlement in the ordered manner that has since become part of modern civilization. Like the settlements established in Scotland during the Improvement movement, each of these military plantations was a small city in microcosm. If Roman colonization had taken root, many of the forts would doubtless have developed into full-scale towns.

The permanent forts were of standard pattern, adapted to local sites. In plan they were rectangles with curved corners, and a gateway in each side leading to roads that crossed in the centre. Typically, at the centre stood the headquarters building, flanked by the commander's house and granaries. Barrack blocks were set in gridded rows, along with hospital, baths, latrines and so forth. Some buildings were of stone but most were of timber and wattle-and-daub, externally and internally plastered, with shingled or thatched roofs.

These plan features are seen at their most developed in Inchtuthil [10], which covers 22 hectares. This was the empire's most northerly legionary fort, and one of the few whose entire layout survives free of built encroachment today. The complex was constructed in two phases, with the initial earth ramparts partly refaced in stone by around AD 86. The buildings inside were timber-framed; they included barracks, six granaries, several officers' houses, a hospital (planned in ward blocks around a courtyard) and a workshop. Subordinate structures nearby include a vast construction camp and a stone quarry. In 86 or 87

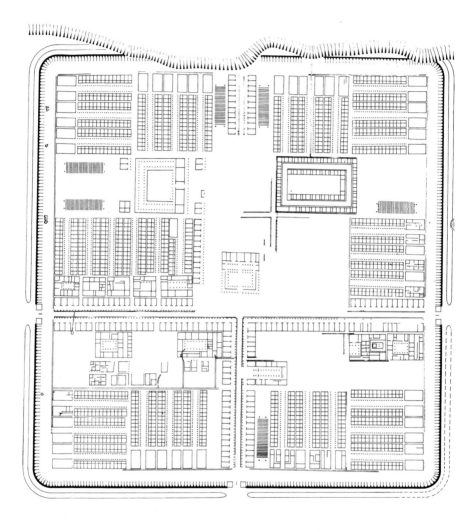

the Scottish garrison was abruptly withdrawn, and construction was abandoned.

The second invasion, in 140, entailed the building of many forts, roughly up to the Tay. The Antonine Wall was erected across the Forth–Clyde gap, fortifying the isthmus on the same principle as Hadrian's Wall in Northumberland – a development of the Gask Frontier concept with the addition of a fixed wall – and comprisingd around sixteen forts and forty fortlets, together with harbours and other settlements, linked by a turf wall on a wide stone base. Some of the forts were of considerable elaboration: that at Bearsden, Dunbartonshire, had a full-scale bath-house with plastered walls and glazed windows.

The Antonine military infrastructure was supplemented by innovations in civilian agricultural building. North of the Forth and especially in Angus and Perthshire, a new Iron Age building type emerged at around this time: the 'souterrain', seemingly a kind of monumental, stone-lined underground grain store used by farmers to house bulk foodstuffs, perhaps for sale to the twelve-thousand-strong Roman forces. These curved tunnel-like spaces were usually around 1.5 metres (5 feet) high and flanked by larger, stone-walled chambers. Often, they were attached to dwellings: at Newmill, Perthshire, a large roundhouse of the 1st century AD was partly encircled by a souterrain, entered from inside the house.

The final two campaigns, under Septimius Severus, again advanced north up the eastern flank. The force was now far larger, and some of the largest temporary camps may date from this time; other sites were re-used. On the death of the Emperor in 211, however, most of the troops abruptly retreated to Hadrian's Wall.

What was the architectural legacy of the Romans in Scotland? In the period immediately following the final withdrawal in the 4th century, there were only indirect traces of the ordered Roman ethos of rectangular buildings and settlements: for a time, the old Iron Age patterns simply resumed, including the building of roundhouses and the occupation of hillforts. But there persisted a more general linkage to the Roman cultural legacy, not least through the use of Latin script, and the continuing awareness of Roman concepts of Europe-wide political power and order, which would indirectly facilitate the spread of Christianity and its built monuments. More negative was the Romans' first establishment of the idea that 'Caledonia' was a peripheral or remote place – an idea that would persist until the early 19th century.

10 Inchtuthil, Perthshire: plan of the Roman legionary fortress, c. AD 80–87. The most northerly legionary fort in the empire, it was abandoned uncompleted, as shown by the open spaces on the plan. The timber-framed structures inside the walls included barracks, service buildings such as granaries, and a hospital; there was also a brick-built bath-house. The headquarters block was in the centre.

In the wake of the Romans, the present-day territory of Scotland was at first sharply divided around the Forth–Clyde line: to the south were the more Romanized Britons, while to the north were the enemies of Rome, whom the Romans referred to disparagingly as the 'painted men' – the Picts. These were still essentially amorphous tribal groupings. However, under the indirect influence of Roman political concepts, a new pattern of discrete but fluctuating kingdoms, led by warrior-rulers and aristocracies, began to emerge. In some cases, these overlapped the present boundaries of Scotland. In the west, there were close links between the expansionist, Gaelic-speaking Argyll kingdom of Dál Riata and north-western Ireland. From the south-east came a wave of Germanic Anglian invaders, who formed a separate kingdom of Bernicia or Northumbria centred in present-day north-east England. The Picts evolved into a loose confederation of at least seven tribal thanages or kingdoms, stretching from the Forth to Orkney and Shetland. The territories and relative power of Britons, Picts, Dál Riata and Northumbrians fluctuated at each other's expense, until, between 793 and 904, a new wave of seaborne invaders and settlers swept in from Scandinavia, wresting the northern and western extremities and islands from the Picts. In response, from the mid-9th century, the Picts and Dál Riata gradually merged to form a single Gaelic kingdom of 'Alba' – precursor of the kingdom of Scotland.

Superimposed on this bewildering human mosaic, and interdependent with it, was the religious framework of Western 'Christendom' – a term which, during the Middle Ages, meant roughly what we today call 'Europe'. Western Christianity was the heir of the Roman Empire in its aspiration to a single, universal Church: until the late Middle Ages, its claims to an overarching sovereignty under the Pope in Rome restricted the potential autonomy of any ruler or nation. However, the Church was also riven from the beginning by its own factional and geographical divisions. From the 5th to the 9th centuries, the four territories of the Picts, Northumbrians, Britons and Dál Riata all witnessed an intermittent proselytizing competition between 'Celtic' and 'Roman' branches of Christianity – the former introduced to Scotland by St Columba in 563. The conclusion was a gradual merger of the two, paralleling in some ways the emergence of the kingdom of Alba.

The surviving architectural legacy of this period is fragmentary in the extreme, but its ruling figures were also celebrated in another, more literal type of 'monument' – the often grandiose sculptured stones that dotted the landscape of early medieval Britain and Ireland, in an insular offshoot of the Roman tradition of large-scale commemorative sculpture. Here the chief division was between the Celtic and Northumbrian freestanding crosses [13], found especially in religious contexts, and the diverse Pictish tradition. The latter began around the 6th century in the Pictish pre-Christian era, using incised geometrical symbols and stylized animals and figurative scenes. The Pictish tradition reached its climax between the 8th and the 10th centuries, with a new phase of explicitly Christian stones, many carved in relief with a cross on one side and symbol decoration on the other: these showed a convergence between Pictish and Roman imagery.

Centres of kingship

The early kingdoms developed in the 6th and 7th centuries around a decentralized pattern of royal fortresses, located on outcrops, often on the coast. For example, the Argyll centres of Dál Riata included Dunadd [11], Dunollie and Dunaverty, all sited on crags (as their very names imply); the British kingdom of Strathclyde was centred on the north Clydeside rock of Dumbarton; the Gododdin of the south-east had Edinburgh rock as a fortress. The Picts initially followed the same pattern in their regional tribal thanages, each of which typically had a grand royal ceremonial stronghold, and farmsteads scattered in the countryside around. In the lands of the Picts and Dál Riata and in Viking territories the roundhouse pattern began to be replaced by the indirectly 'Roman' tradition of rectangular-plan houses. But from around the 7th or 8th century, as we will see, the Picts developed a new and more sophisticated pattern based in the farming lowlands of 'Fortriu' (Perthshire), and focused on a single unfortified royal 'palace' at Forteviot, near the former Gask Frontier, subsequently taken over as the chief centre of Alba. This southern part of Pictland, rather than the Clyde–Forth isthmus, would remain the most important part of the country until at least the 13th century.

In most of these early territories, the chief fortresses followed the same basically hierarchical pattern, with an acropolis citadel and terraced, ramparted enclosures clustered around. In some cases, settlements were apparently given greater status by siting them near to pre-existing ancient ritual and ceremonial sites, such as stone circles. The fortresses themselves were sometimes re-used Iron Age forts, and sometimes on completely new sites, chosen as appropriate settings for kingship. Perhaps the most important example of the former is Dunadd [11], a Dál Riata royal centre of the 6th–8th centuries, located near an excellent anchorage and beside the major Neolithic and Bronze Age ritual complex at Kilmartin Glen. Here an Iron Age site on a prominent rock was re-occupied as a royal 'inauguration site' (for use in the ceremonial acclamation or rulers), with two carved footprints cut into the summit bedrock, together with other inscribed designs. The acropolis incorporated a 4th–5th century oval-plan fort, which was successively enlarged in the 7th–8th centuries with domestic and ceremonial buildings, and workshops for the manufacture of luxury metalwork and jewelry. Pictish fortresses of the 4th–8th centuries are similar in pattern. The colossal 4th–6th-century promontory fort of Burghead, near Elgin (Moray), adjoining a harbour possibly used as a base by Pictish warships, comprised an agglomeration of rampart enclosures, built around a heavy timber frame and following Roman precedent with timber

11 Dunadd, Argyll: plan of the Dál Riata royal centre of the 6th–8th century, which re-occupied the site of an Iron Age hillfort. Multiple platforms constructed during the extended development of this 'acropolis' can be seen, in addition to the oval 'Upper Fort' at the highest point of the site.

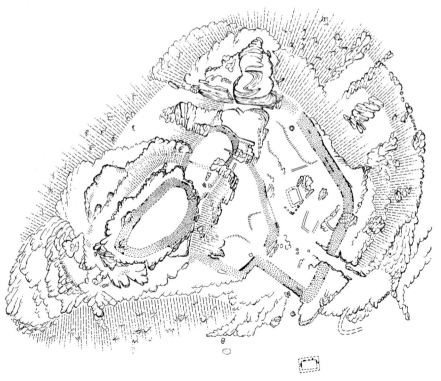

superstructures, unusually employing nails. The slightly later site of Dundurn, in Strathearn, possibly dates from the time of consolidation of Pictish power in the fertile south. It, too, comprises a stone- and timber-walled citadel, rebuilt in numerous phases in the 6th–8th centuries, including terraces and ramparts of sometimes enormous thickness, and a platform possibly used for the inauguration of the Strathearn rulers.

The only palace from this period whose rough location has been discovered was the most important of all: Forteviot, the focal site of the late Pictish kings of Fortriu and the first royal centre of the macAilpín dynasty's unified kingship of Alba. In a significant move away from the hillfort tradition, an unfortified Pictish royal centre was first established here in the 7th or 8th century. By the death of King Cinaed macAilpín in 858 the complex included a royal 'palacium' and a great hall, both probably of timber, and a richly decorated church or chapel. In the vicinity were two important freestanding crosses – monuments to the interrelated power of king and Church. The site was probably chosen because of the presence of a (now vanished) Neolithic ritual landscape, including a stone circle – a common trend for royal sites in Scotland and Ireland from before the 8th century, and the beginning of the concept of associative 'historic landscape'. Although it continued in royal use until at least the 12th century, almost all trace of this Carolingian-style palace has now disappeared, with a few exceptions including a fragment of the 8th- or 9th-century church [16] and the Dupplin Cross, a freestanding monument of c. 820 with carvings that depict the military victories of Custantin (Constantine), King of Fortriu and Dál Riata, who is shown as a triumphal equestrian figure in a mixture of kingly militarism and Christianity that brings us squarely into the medieval world. By 906, a new royal inauguration site in Perthshire was adopted by the kings of Alba (or Scots), at Scone, where an earthwork hill, the 'Hill of Belief', saw the proclamation of new religious laws by King Constantine II and the Bishop of St Andrews.

Religious Building: from Iona to St Andrews
The same multi-centred pattern is found in the religious buildings of early Scotland. There was a sharp contrast between the Irish monastic system imported by St Columba or Colum Cille to Iona in 563, with its combination of pastoral activity and seclusion in remote monasteries and hermitages, and the vast, formal diocesan hierarchy of the Roman Church, with its bishops and cathedral seats, and its potentially more ambitious architecture of grand

basilican churches. Spatially, these two rival interpretations of Western Christianity developed their own Scottish centres, with the more ascetic and eremitical Irish Church establishing numerous foundations in Dál Riata, and the Roman Church setting up new centres in Pictland, including the pilgrimage site of St Andrews in Fife [18]. From the 8th century, there was the further complication of the 'Culdees' (Céli Dé), a reformed, austere order imported from Ireland via Iona, and ultimately assimilated into Roman monasticism in the 12th century.

At first there was very little practical difference in architectural outcomes, as the buildings actually erected in any region were modest, single-cell structures, and almost all traces of them have in any case vanished (unlike the monumental sculptures which often substituted for formal churches as the focus of wayside worship, creating a local religious landscape). Excavations at Whithorn in the south-west revealed a 7th-century or earlier monastic settlement with multiple churches, but the same site has also produced the earliest known Christian monument in Scotland, the mid-5th-century Latinus stone. Thus a Romanized Christian lay community clearly existed here at that time. At Ardwall Island in Kirkcudbrightshire a 6th-century cemetery was augmented in the following century by a timber oratory and, in the 8th century, by a stone chapel. In Pictland, royal land was said to have been granted at Abernethy to St Brigid, who sent the Abbess Darlugdach to build a church there in 485; this church may have been a wooden chapel, and a predecessor of the round tower and modern parish church (dedicated to St Bride) built on the same site.

The cradle of the Celtic Church in Britain was the isle of Iona [12, 13], where a monastery was first established by Columba in 563. It reached the peak of its influence in the time of the scholar-statesman Adomnán (abbot from 779 to 804), a key figure in the reconciliation of the Celtic and Roman Churches. During the 9th century it was repeatedly devastated by Viking raids, but it remained the burial place of Scottish kings until the late 11th century. In keeping with the monastic search for isolation, the island site, although flat and protected, was one of the most remote in Dál Riata. In Columba's time, a variety of ephemeral timber and wattle buildings, rectangular or circular in plan – churches, dwellings, workshops, barns and kilns – were erected within the outer walled boundary. In his Life of Columba, Adomnán refers to numerous buildings, though insufficiently precisely to allow identification: they include a main church with linear plan, and a wattle-and-timber 'magna domus' or common

12 Iona: aerial view of the area within the *vallum*, which, in the time of St Columba, contained a variety of ephemeral timber and rubble buildings. In the foreground is the later Benedictine monastery (mostly of the 13th and 20th centuries). At the upper right is the early 13th-century Augustinian nunnery. The modern village is at upper centre.

refectory. It is clear, however, that even in this remote spot there was direct knowledge of the earliest Mediterranean churches: Adomnán's book *De Locis Sanctis* ('On the Holy Places') contains a careful plan of the Church of the Holy Sepulchre in Jerusalem – Scotland's earliest architectural drawing. The oldest surviving building in the Iona complex is of the 9th century or later: 'St Columba's Shrine', a tiny stone-built structure abutting the façade of the early 13th-century Benedictine abbey church. [13].

In addition to Iona, other lesser hermitages were scattered across even remoter extremities of the west coast. Even on the island of North Rona, 70 kilometres (43 miles) from the nearest land at the far north of the Hebrides, substantial traces survive of an early Christian hermitage, including an oval enclosure and *vallum* (boundary ditch) containing a rectangular drystone-built oratory. But by the 9th century, in response to the Viking attacks, the religious focus was shifting south-eastwards: in 849, the

13 Iona: the Benedictine abbey, built *c.* 1200 on the
site of Columba's community, and later enlarged
(and reconstructed in 1938–65 by Ian G. Lindsay).
The small pitched-roof structure to the left of the
west end of the abbey church is the 9th-century
'St Columba's Shrine'. The two monumental crosses
visible are (left) a reproduction of the mid-8th-
century St John's Cross (the widest in span of any
Early Christian cross in Britain or Ireland), and (right)
St Martin's Cross, probably of the late 8th century.

relics of Columba were divided between Kells in Ireland and Dunkeld in Perthshire, where a new church (now vanished) was built to house them.

From the late 7th century, the Columban Church had gradually accommodated itself to the Roman system, with its provision for closer links between king and Church, and by at least the 8th century the outlines of a diocesan and parish system had begun to emerge in Pictland/Alba, with the founding of bishoprics and monasteries at Dunkeld and St Andrews. This gradual Romanization of the Church, together with the southward shift in Pictish political power to the lowlands around Forteviot, was reflected in a subtle change of architectural direction. The link became very clear in 711, when the Pictish King Nechtan sent to Ceolfrid, the foremost Northumbrian abbot, for guidance on the Roman conventions of tonsure and religious dating, and, according to Bede, also asked him to send 'architects [or masons] who might build a stone church, in the Roman manner', promising that he would dedicate it to St Peter. In his drive to open the Pictish Church, and society, to the wider world of Christendom, Nechtan was seeking something different from the earth and timber construction of the present – something akin to the dressed

14 Restenneth Priory, Angus: the lower portion of the tower is probably of 10th-century date, rather than 8th-century as it would be if it was from King Nechtan's church. The upper part of the tower is 12th-century, and the broach spire 15th-century. The chancel was consecrated in 1243 when the church had become that of an Augustinian priory.

stonework and regular plans of contemporary Continental architecture, inspired both by Roman grandeur and by complex biblical symbolism. It is unclear where, or whether, stone buildings were actually erected in response to Nechtan's initiative. The much-rebuilt tower of Restenneth Priory in Angus [14] has often been identified as the stone church commissioned by Nechtan – especially as the place-name of 'Egglespether' (St Peter's Church) was recorded in the vicinity in the 12th century – but it is probably of 10th- rather than 8th-century date. Possibly dating from the 8th century is the earliest surviving fragment of a formal stone church, a sculptured round-arched monolithic door lintel excavated within the Fortriu palace site at Forteviot [16], which apparently depicts at its apex a paschal lamb. If it is earlier than, or contemporary with, the Dupplin Cross of c. 820, it may commemorate King Oengus II, who is associated with the foundation legend of St Andrews.

By the 10th or early 11th century, a number of quite ambitious church buildings of dressed stone or ashlar had begun to materialize in the ecclesiastical centres of this former Pictish heartland. From the surviving fragments, they were planned in a linear, accretional way, with chambers or towers strung out in line, or campanile-like towers on their own. Belfries had a special status at this time, owing to their importance in signalling the passage of sacred time. Two tall round towers, at Brechin in Angus and Abernethy in Perthshire, hint at the continuing links between Roman and Columban/Irish Christianity: they are early Romanesque-influenced versions of the round towers built in Ireland from Viking times to provide broch-like security for church functions such as libraries. The Brechin tower [15], just over 26 metres (87 feet) high (excluding the later spire), with its high-quality coursed masonry and its doorway with zoomorphic motifs in the style of the Pictish cross-head inside the cathedral, may date from the late 10th century: it certainly existed by 1017, when it survived the sacking of Brechin by the Danes. The doorway is made up of a curved monolith, as at Forteviot [16], set on monolithic jambs. The Abernethy tower, built probably in the 11th century at the centre of a former Pictish bishopric, has a round-headed doorway with a Crucifixion and various Pictish-style anthromorphic figures.

A number of tall rectangular towers with two-light arched belfry windows, some possibly of 11th-century date, survive in the same area: for example in Perthshire at Dunblane (abutted by the later cathedral) [17] and in Fife at Markinch Church (granted

16 The 'Forteviot Arch', possibly of 8th- or early 9th-century date, excavated within the Pictish Fortriu palace site at Forteviot, Perthshire. It is the arched top to a door (cf. that at Brechin, ill. 15). At the centre – the fragment is here tipped slightly to the right – is a paschal lamb; to the left of it is what has been variously interpreted as a standing king or a cross. The hooded figures carrying staffs to right and left (the latter accompanied by an animal) are again the subject of conjecture.

opposite
15 The round tower of Brechin Cathedral, Angus, possibly of late 10th-century date. The round-headed doorway at the bottom is carved with animal motifs.

to the Culdees of Lochleven by the Bishop of St Andrews in the early 11th century). And in the mid-11th century there existed a single-cell church and tower at Dunfermline in Fife, extended after 1070 by Queen Margaret and later replaced by the present abbey.

The spiritual focus of this network of buildings was St Andrews [18], again in Fife, which had now established itself as the primary religious centre of the former Pictish lands, rivalling the prestige of Iona. St Andrews, or Cennrigmonaid ('Head of the King's Mount' in Gaelic), was a centre of pilgrimage as well as a Culdee monastery and cathedral seat: by the 9th century, the pilgrimage movement had established itself as a focus of vast popular enthusiasm and financial support for Christianity. St Andrews was first mentioned as the seat of an abbot in 747, and by the 12th century there was an extensive religious precinct, ringed by stone crosses and containing seven churches and a 'basilica'. The most magnificent relic of the foundation era is the 'St Andrews Sarcophagus', a shrine-like tomb dating from *c.* 750–850, possibly intended to hold the remains of King Onuist son of Uurguist (d. 761), one of the founders of St Andrews.

At the time, the most important shrine in St Andrews was that which held the relics of the apostle St Andrew, allegedly brought to Scotland by St Regulus, or St Rule. It seems clear from a late 11th-century reference that a church purpose-built to hold these relics had existed for some time on the site; what we now know as St Rule's Church [18] was probably built in the early 11th century. Constructed of close-jointed ashlar masonry of a quality previously unknown in Scotland, St Rule's comprises a tall two-bay rectangular chamber and a sheer western tower with two-light belfry as at Dunblane [17]. It was probably intended as a colossal reliquary, with the tower serving as a landmark for pilgrims to this northern Compostela. In the 12th century, Bishop Robert made further enlargements to convert the pilgrimage church into a cathedral, including a new nave to the west of the tower, and he heightened the arches at either end of the existing church to improve the view of the raised shrine. But it was the earlier construction of a uniquely monumental building to house the saint's relics that represented the culmination of the centuries of effort, by the Picts and their religious and royal successors, to naturalize a 'Roman' stone grandeur in Scotland.

Chapter 2   1100–1560: From Christendom to Kingdom

During the 1st millennium AD, Scotland's patchwork of peoples and kingdoms had existed at one remove from the dominant Continental powers of Christendom and their architectures. In the period covered by this chapter that relative isolation ended. A unified Scottish kingdom was consolidated, against the backdrop of powerful forces from outside, in the shape of centralized Latin Christianity and an expansionist Norman English monarchy. During the 12th and 13th centuries, the authority of kings of Scots existed somewhat in the shadow of these forces, especially of the power of the Church, almost unimaginable today in its overriding, authoritative character. From the 14th century, both these influences declined. Although late medieval Scotland was generally a fairly peaceful place by Continental standards, the 14th century was a sharp exception to this, with its prolonged Wars of Independence – a succession of conflicts with England in which the latter's claims to overlordship over Scotland were resisted. The successful outcome of these wars, led most notably by King Robert the Bruce (r. 1306–29), resulted in a more autonomous relationship vis-à-vis England, and a growing closeness to France, while the increasing challenges to Rome's authority left the Scottish kings able to strike a more self-confident pose. The 1340s also saw the start of two centuries of recurrent plague, greatly accentuating social imbalances between rich and poor.

The architectural effects of these dramatic fluctuations were also clear-cut. Two and a half centuries of sharply differentiated religious and lordly secular building, heavily derivative of Continental and English patterns and dominated by the trans-national requirements of the Church, were followed, after the prolonged devastation of the 14th century, by a very different and distinctive period, in which church building slipped back in relative importance, and was to some extent eclipsed by the secular

19 Elgin Cathedral, Moray: the late 13th-century east end has tiered lancets in the St Andrews tradition (cf. ill. 18) and flanking polygonal buttress-towers.

building types of castles and palaces. From being a very minor player in the world of medieval Gothic, already by the Reformation of 1560 Scotland had become a land of castles – something of great importance for later centuries.

Discipline and Diversity: Abbeys and Cathedrals of the Romanesque Era

During the late 11th and early 12th centuries, a succession of rulers, including Malcolm III (r. 1058–93) and Margaret, and culminating in David I (r. 1124–53), implemented a string of reforms to assert their own power and bring Scotland into alignment with the wider world of Latin Christendom. By the mid-12th century, David (the brother-in-law of Henry I of England) had extended his power into Northumbria and Cumbria, introduced new central and local government régimes based on Anglo-Norman precedents, devoted vast resources to church building and the formation of dioceses and parishes, and founded large numbers of planned towns, or burghs. This process of urbanization would only bear real fruit from the 16th century onwards, since Scotland remained an overwhelmingly rural country for the whole of the Middle Ages. More important in the short term was David's foundation of large numbers of monasteries – the most powerful agency of religious centralization in those years.

The older kind of decentralized Benedictine monasticism had been introduced at Dunfermline by Queen Margaret in the 11th century, but it was the then Prince David who in 1113 founded the first Scottish community of reformed Benedictine monks, at Selkirk (later moved to Kelso in Roxburghshire [20]). On his accession to the throne in 1124, David was patron of at least nine monasteries of different orders in Scotland, and from 1128 he re-founded and largely rebuilt Dunfermline Priory [21] as a grand abbey, which eventually became one of the richest in Scotland, equipped with a royal guesthouse range. The Cistercian order or White Monks reached Scotland in 1136, in a monastery founded by David at Melrose in Roxburghshire, as a daughter house of Rievaulx in Yorkshire. Slightly earlier, in 1120, Alexander II had founded at Scone in Perthshire the first Scottish house of Augustinian canons – a kind of monastery made up of ordained priests. Later Augustinian abbeys founded by David I included Holyrood (1128) [48, 61], Jedburgh, again in Roxburghshire (c. 1138) [22], and Inchcolm in Fife (c. 1153), as well as the cathedral priory of St Andrews (by 1144) [18, 23]. The order of Premonstratensian White Canons, an equivalent of the Cistercian

20 Kelso Abbey, Roxburghshire, founded in 1128: view of the 'westwork' with its tower and transepts. Kelso was one of the foremost monuments of Romanesque architecture in Scotland; the church's unusual double-cross plan included east and west crossings, each with a pyramid-capped tower. It was severely damaged in the 16th century by English invasions.

monks, was established in Scotland at Dryburgh Abbey, Berwickshire, in 1150–52.

These reformed orders were organized in a more disciplined and assertive way than the old Celtic and Culdee communities. Monastic life was dominated by ascetic self-containment, including almost constant services, but some houses also had extensive involvement in the wider community. They busied themselves with farming and the wool trade, and the founding of satellite daughter houses and support of parish churches. The layout of monasteries had become largely stereotyped during the first millennium [23]. It was dominated by the main church building, which was usually designed on a Latin-cross plan, with the choir at the eastern, more ceremonial end, projecting transepts, a belfry tower or towers at the crossing or the west end, and a basilican section, with lower aisles flanking a high nave. To the south of the church was an arcaded square courtyard, or cloister – an enlarged version of the Roman peristyle – from which opened the main spaces of daily monastic life, including the chapter house (the community's council chamber), the dormitory, and the refectory, a large collective dining hall. There was often also a great variety of other ancillary buildings, within a large walled precinct. The different orders of monks or canons each had their own distinctive architectural emphases, faithfully reflected in their Scottish offshoots. For example, the more ascetic Cistercians originally favoured relatively simple plans and condemned bell towers, while the more ceremony-loving orders required more complex church plans with chapels and ambulatories (passages encircling the east end). But what they had in common was far more important than these variations.

This new and more coordinated religious ethos was matched, from the 11th century, by a new architectural approach across western Christendom, including Scotland – the architecture we today call Romanesque. Like the architecture of the Carolingian Renaissance, it was inspired by the round-arched buildings of ancient Rome, but it used these and early Christian precedents more freely, although there was occasionally a literal evocation of classical forms, as for instance in a 12th-century Corinthian capital at Douglas Church, Lanarkshire. More important was a new, three-dimensional and integrated approach to planning and construction, with the use of multiple or engaged orders to model the wall planes, and vaulting and tall steeples soaring above. A typical Romanesque great church interior was a tall three-storey space with arcades separating the central vessel from the aisles,

21 Dunfermline Abbey, Fife: view looking west in the nave, c. 1130–40. The piers in the foreground have incised decoration on the model of that in Durham Cathedral.

and above them a triforium gallery and windowed clearstorey [21]. At Cistercian abbeys the more austere philosophy usually demanded a simpler, square east end, a low belfry, and timber roofs.

Although certain canonical monuments such as the Church of the Holy Sepulchre in Jerusalem and St Peter's in Rome had a pervasive authority, Romanesque was very much a style of regional diversity, with the influence of major monuments radiating into the surrounding areas. For Scotland (and Northumbria) in the age of David I, the main regional conduit for these wider influences was the Anglo-Norman style of the vast new Durham Cathedral, built from the late 11th century. For the nave of his new showpiece abbey church at Dunfermline [21], built c. 1130–40, David I imported masons from Durham, and some columns of the nave arcade echo Durham (but at half scale) in their zig-zag and spiral incised patterning, with cushion capitals. Dunfermline introduced to Scotland the typical three-storey Romanesque church section. There were other regional styles of Romanesque in Scotland. For example, the detailing of the mid-12th century choir of Jedburgh [22], with its intermediate gallery stage recessed into the arcade arches, reflects patterns at churches in the south and west of England, such as Romsey. A more austere, small-windowed pattern, associated with Irish masons, was found on the west coast. A notable example of this was the new Benedictine abbey and nunnery at Iona, on the site of Columba's community, built on a simple cruciform plan c. 1200 and subsequently enlarged with choir aisles, a cloister and refectory, and a low, massive tower and cloister; the present-day appearance of the complex is largely the result of a reconstruction and restoration of 1938-65 by Ian G. Lindsay. [12, 13].

22 Jedburgh Abbey, Roxburghshire: detail of the choir, mid-12th-century. The galleries are set within a two-storey arcade – an unusual system found also in the south and west of England. The complexity of this arrangement contrasts with the flush surfaces and sharply demarcated storeys of Dunfermline (ill. 21).

This increased discipline and coordination of architecture was paralleled by a more general increase in the sheer quantity, scale and material quality of church building, fuelled financially by the soaring popularity of relics and shrines – although, unlike England, France, Italy and Germany, the Church in Scotland could not generally afford to build abbeys and cathedrals on the largest scale. Over the century up until 1130, stone construction had spread to almost all new church buildings, and the increasingly monumental abbeys and churches were designed methodically by master masons using practical systems of constructional geometry. With the aid of nothing more than compasses and a rope to trace out circles and rotating squares, complex plans could be laid out and elevations and vaults projected from them. But the layout and design of buildings were conditioned not just by practical use and design geometry, but also by symbolic or allegorical biblical associations, evoking Jerusalem indirectly for those who could not themselves make the pilgrimage. Unlike modern architects, medieval masons were concerned not so much with space in the abstract as with the symbolic force of thresholds, divisions and façades.

In their scale and ambition, Scotland's abbeys were matched by the cathedrals, the centres of a complex diocesan system that had emerged from the 8th century, and had been extended under the kings of the late 11th and 12th centuries. It was David's ultimate strategy to block the claims of the Archbishop of York to supremacy by establishing an archbishopric at St Andrews; that aim was only realized in 1472. In contrast to an abbey church, a cathedral needed to provide large spaces and numbers of altars for lay folk, and thus could potentially become quite large; however, the ancillary buildings, such as bishops' palaces and manses, were less stereotyped than in the abbeys. Most Scottish cathedrals were run by secular (non-monastic) canons, and were thus strongly differentiated from the religious houses. In the larger and more developed cathedrals, in contrast to the monastic churches, there was a strong differentiation between the nave, for the lay folk (often boasting a proliferation of chapels), and the choir for the clergy, marked off by screen and stalls. But in common with the abbey churches, the crossing was often accentuated by projecting transepts and a tower: the most ceremonial area, the chancel, was around the high altar, sometimes flanked by processual aisles, chapels and ambulatory.

The greatest Scottish cathedral of the period (and the only one of similar size to the largest English and Continental

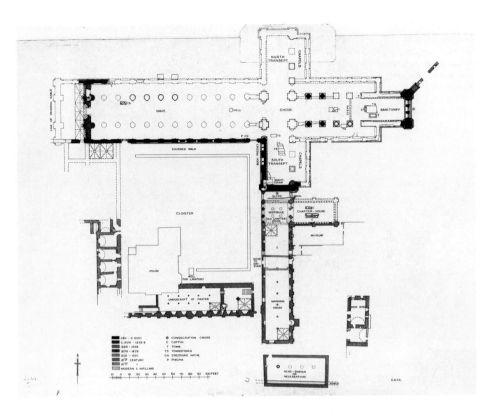

23 Plan of the ruins of the cathedral priory of St Andrews, Fife. Surviving elements (cf. ill. 18) are shown in black. Note the enormous length of the church, begun in 1160, and the extensive cloister to the south, mostly of mid-13th-century date. The chapter house lies off the eastern range of the cloister, which also contained a 'warming-house', and which supported the dormitory above. To the south of this was the detached reredorter (latrine) block. The southern range of the cloister contained the refectory. The remnants of the west range comprise tunnel-vaulted ruins of unspecified purpose.

examples) was an exception to this pattern of management: that at St Andrews, founded in 1160 by Malcolm IV (r. 1153–65), adjacent to St Rule's [18, 23]. Almost nothing of this great church survives today. It was a hybrid of cathedral and priory church, as it served both the diocese and the priory of Augustinian canons located around a cloister to its south. It was correspondingly vast in scale, nearly 120 metres (355 feet) long, and all in dressed ashlar. Construction proceeded from the east for nearly a century, and it was eventually consecrated in 1318. Fragments of the Romanesque architecture are incorporated in the remaining ruins, notably the sanctuary east gable (originally provided with three tiers of round-arched windows) and much of the remaining southern walling, with intersecting blind arcading at ground level (e.g. on the south transept); in a foretaste of the 'Gothic' architecture of the 13th century, there were probably pointed arches in the choir arcades.

Some of the other Romanesque cathedrals were on a much smaller scale. For instance, the seat of the bishopric of Moray, re-established c. 1107, was Birnie, a very modest mid-12th-century

church which still survives intact, with its nave and lower chancel, separated by a round archway. Such cathedrals hardly differed from the early parish churches built following David's establishment of a full parochial system. Examples of those are Leuchars in Fife (built by c. 1185) [24] and Dalmeny in West Lothian; both had tall aisleless naves, narrower square chancels and semi-circular apses; similarities to Dunfermline in the use of ornament suggest that the Durham masons were employed here too.

The most complete surviving Romanesque cathedral in Scotland, and the earliest commenced to a single unified design, is St Magnus's Cathedral, Kirkwall, Orkney [25]. This building was not, strictly speaking, 'Scottish' at all when first built, as Orkney up to the 13th century formed part of the Norse kingdoms of the North Sea, and the diocese of Trondheim; between the 13th and 15th centuries it was ruled by a succession of Scottish earls, and passed finally to the Crown in 1470. Orkney had witnessed the building of a number of unusual churches in the 12th century, including one with a round tower at Egilsay, and one with a circular nave (doubtless evoking the Holy Sepulchre in Jerusalem) at Orphir. St Magnus's was begun c. 1137 at the instigation of Earl Rognvald Kali Kolsson, nephew of St Magnus, on a cruciform plan with crossing tower, and the choir was completed in a few years. Again, the detailing of the Romanesque work suggests the influence of Durham, for example in the original liturgical arrangement of the east end, with an ambulatory to give access to the tomb of St Magnus; but the use of red and white

25 St Magnus's Cathedral, Kirkwall, Orkney, begun c. 1137. This view, from the north-west, shows the original nave and transept. The crossing was rebuilt in the mid-13th century.

polychromatic stonework was an idiosyncratic – perhaps Mediterranean-inspired? – variation. Later, in the mid-13th century, to provide a more illustrious setting for Magnus's shrine, the area immediately around the crossing was partly rebuilt and the choir was extended to the east and given a giant east window. The nave was built in a plainer Romanesque style in several phases from the mid-12th century to around 1500. The 12th century also saw the construction next door of a hall, similar to the great stone hall built in Bergen by King Haakon of Norway.

Pointed Arches, Round Arches: Later Medieval Church Architecture
From the early 12th century, beginning probably in the French abbey of Cluny, the round-arched, massive Romanesque was gradually replaced by the slenderer and bolder Gothic style of pointed arches. Initially, Gothic was a strikingly unified

26 Glasgow Cathedral: the site of the tomb of St Kentigern or Mungo, focus of the vaulted undercroft, after c. 1240.

27 Glasgow Cathedral, seen from the south-east. The building is largely 13th-century in date. This view shows the taller roofs of the choir (foreground) and nave, and the gabled south transept, projecting above the level of the continuous aisles and eastern ambulatory to give a compact rectangular plan. The central tower is of 15th-century date; two other (asymmetrical) towers at the west end were destroyed in 1846–48. The site, steeply sloping to the east, made possible an extensive vaulted lower church (see ill. 26) occupying the full area of the building east of the crossing, as well as the only completed floor of the unfinished 13th-century Blackadder Aisle, (or chapel) projecting southwards from the south transept. (Visible behind to the right is the Glasgow Royal Infirmary by James Miller, 1901–14.)

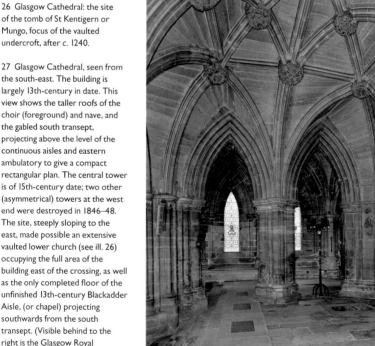

phenomenon, radiating outwards from France right across Latin Christendom by the early 13th century, especially through the influence of the religious orders. The pointed arch first arrived in Scotland around 1160, probably at St Andrews, and around 1170 was introduced by the Augustinians at Jedburgh Abbey. As in England, in Scotland early Gothic was expressed in otherwise heavy and traditional structures, initially with single lancet windows, set, sometimes in groups, in thick walls, but by the time of 13th-century structures such as Glasgow Cathedral, piers were made up of clustered shafts rather than cylindrical columns. The Rayonnant Gothic of the mid-13th-century Ile-de-France, with its slender piers, delicate tracery and high rib vaults supported by external flying buttresses, became almost an international style for

great churches, but its influence was little felt in Scotland, where full-blooded Gothic was a relatively short-lived and weak movement.

The most important and unified monument of the relatively short period of Gothic ascendancy in Scotland is Glasgow Cathedral [27]. The first church on the site was consecrated in 1136, but what now exists is a harmonious 13th-century design, influenced by English precedents such as Rievaulx Abbey or Lincoln Cathedral. The nave was laid out c. 1200, and around 1240 Bishop Bondington conceived the wider vision of a grand pilgrimage church, focused on the tomb of St Kentigern or Mungo, which was given a dramatic setting in a vast columned undercroft below the choir [26] – an arrangement made possible by the steeply sloping site. Overall, the plan of the main building is contained within a single rectangle, without projecting transepts: the aisles are continuous from west to east. At Elgin in Moray, a cathedral of similar size was built in two stages in the 13th century, beginning with an aisled nave, twin western towers and a short choir. The choir was extended and an extra set of aisles added round the whole church after 1270; the surviving east front [19] features two tiers of grouped lancets (perpetuating a by then long-established tradition, as at St Andrews and Arbroath a century before), topped by a round window and flanked by massive octagonal buttresses. And at Dunblane in Perthshire, a more modest new cathedral was built from around 1240 by Bishop Clement adjacent to the earlier tower [17]. It has an aisleless choir and aisled nave, but no transepts; a two-storey chapter house and sacristy were built on the north side of the choir. The nave west gable is specially distinctive, with three equal-size giant traceried lancets framed by deep buttresses.

The evolution of this worthy but modest regional offshoot of Gothic was interrupted by over a century of intermittent warfare with England, lasting from 1296 to the early 15th century. Scotland and England were on opposite sides of the great Papal Schism of 1378–1417, and during that time religious buildings throughout southern Scotland became legitimate military targets – although the extent of the damage was much exaggerated by Church and military propagandists. The growing sense of national identity increasingly affected the once tranquil Church in Scotland. Many of the historians who now shaped the founding myths of modern Scotland were churchmen. They included John Barbour, archdeacon of Aberdeen and writer of *Bruce* in the 1370s, and Walter Bower, Abbot of Inchcolm from 1418 and author of the

Scotichronicon (completed 1437). By the end of the 15th century, there were attempts to develop a separate Scottish liturgy.

In general, the 14th century saw growing regional differences within European Gothic, so it was unsurprising that Scottish and English church architecture now rapidly diverged. England launched into the flat rectilinear Perpendicular style, while Scotland gradually developed a new style with affinities both to earlier Romanesque churches and to contemporary castles. The potential for divergence was presaged within the single complex of Melrose Abbey, when it was rebuilt after its destruction by the English king, Richard II, in 1385. Work began in 1389 while still in English hands, with the choir and parts of the transepts designed in the Perpendicular style, but by around 1400 a new French mason, Jean Morow, was at work, inserting south transept windows with flowing tracery reminiscent of contemporary French work [28].

Large-scale building was resumed across Scotland from around 1400 under the new Stewart dynasty (the spelling of this dynastic name was changed to the supposedly more French-looking 'Stuart' in the mid-16th century). The early 15th century saw the rapid establishment of a new and distinctive style of church architecture, with heavy masonry walls, massive circular columns, round-arched or simple pointed windows with thick bar tracery, and barrel vaults. The inspiration seems to have been a combination of 13th-century round-pillared churches in the Low Countries and the castle tradition in Scotland itself, to which special prestige already attached. In view of the general accentuation of regional styles in the late Middle Ages, it would be quite wrong to see this new manner as a political or nationalist move in the modern sense. But interestingly, one of its earliest appearances was at Inchcolm Abbey, rebuilt between 1394 and 1449 by Abbot Lawrence and his successor, Abbot Bower, following repeated English attacks: the squat, somewhat fortified-looking group comprised a cruciform church with tunnel vaulting, and an Augustinian monastery with unusual inset cloister. At Dunkeld Cathedral [29], the nave, begun in 1406 by the Paris-educated Bishop Robert Cardeny and completed in 1464 by Bishop Thomas Lauder, was treated in a strongly horizontal manner, with round piers carrying a massive round-arched triforium, a little like a Roman aqueduct. Cardeny also built a castellated bishop's palace, while Lauder built a four-storey bell tower and inserted a huge six-light window into the west gable of the church.

29 Dunkeld Cathedral, Perthshire: the nave, of 1406–64, has idiosyncratic semi-circular triforium arches tightly squeezed between arcade and clearstorey. We are looking west, towards the north aisle and north-west tower.

Perhaps the most characteristic example of the 'castle style' of late medieval church architecture is St Machar's Cathedral, Aberdeen, built in the late 14th and early 15th centuries. The choir and central tower do not survive. The nave is a simpler and earlier version of Dunkeld in rough granite, again with circular piers (the crossing piers have clear Netherlandish precedents); it is surmounted by a flat timber ceiling of c. 1520 painted with royal and ecclesiastical heraldic motifs. Most striking of all is the west façade [30], with a central row of seven lancets (with depressed

30 St Machar's Cathedral, Aberdeen, late 14th and 15th centuries. The west front is marked by a row of seven tall lancets and castle-like towers.

round heads) flanked by fortress-like towers crowned with machicolation and topped by stumpy spires. Many monastic complexes also now began to resemble secular palaces: for example, the Tironensian abbey of Arbroath in Angus was extended in the 15th and early 16th centuries, with additional communal buildings, a tall precinct wall with machicolation and corner tower, and a symmetrical, almost classical, galleried extension of the abbot's house.

Collegiate and Burgh Churches
In Scotland's late medieval church architecture, the most important building types were in many ways not the cathedrals or abbeys, but churches of medium size, stemming from the increasing prosperity of the towns or from the establishment of

many new 'colleges' – foundations of priests dedicated to prayer for the salvation of the founding patron, often in association with some sort of charitable activity, such as education. By the time of the Reformation, about forty collegiate churches existed, most of them built in the 15th century. They are usually rectangular or cruciform in plan, often with a polygonal apse. Many were left incomplete after the patron's immediate requirements had been satisfied. This Continental feature was possibly introduced to Scotland at the collegiate church of St Salvator, St Andrews [31], built by Bishop James Kennedy from c. 1450, with a partly ribbed barrel vault and a tall, austere tower echoing that of St Rule's [18]; Kennedy's canopied tomb survived the Reformation. The same general arrangement was followed at the chapel of King's College, Aberdeen, built in 1500–1509 by Bishop William Elphinstone.

The most richly endowed collegiate chapels were often of idiosyncratic design. The two-storey chapel royal of James III

31 St Salvator's Collegiate Church, St Andrews, Fife, begun c. 1450: the south façade and tower. (From R. W. Billings, *Baronial and Ecclesiastical Antiquities of Scotland*, 1845–52)

(r. 1460–88) at Restalrig, outside Edinburgh (1487), has a hexagonal plan, doubtless to recall the Church of the Holy Sepulchre in Jerusalem; James III's friend, the traveller and cleric Anselm Adornes, had completed the octagonal Jerusalemkerk in Bruges in the 1450s. Trinity College Church, Edinburgh, established in 1460 by James II's widow, Mary of Gueldres, had unusually rich ornamentation and fittings, including an altarpiece of the late 1470s by the Flemish master Hugo van der Goes (now in the National Gallery of Scotland). Only the choir and transepts, and a fragment of a saddleback crossing tower, were completed; the church was demolished in 1848 for the expansion of Waverley Station, and partly rebuilt nearby in 1872 by the architect John Lessels (1808–83). By far the most richly decorated collegiate foundation was Roslin in Midlothian [32], established by William Sinclair, Earl of Orkney and Caithness, and probably built between the late 1440s and the 1460s. Only the five-bay choir, ringed by diminutive flying buttresses, and the transept east wall were completed. Like Glasgow Cathedral, the choir has aisles, a straight east end with an ambulatory, and a crypt, but these are treated with an exotic ornateness found in the late Gothic architecture of countries such as Spain and Portugal, but otherwise unknown in Scotland. The precise inspiration of such elements as the Apprentice Pillar, a fluted pillar with spiralled overlay, is unknown, although various Iberian and Mediterranean sources, as well as Old Testament symbolism, have been suggested. Some features of Roslin, such as the segmental coffered choir vault and the flat aisle lintels, have more classical overtones.

The building of relatively large burgh churches was a mark of the growing confidence of the towns, especially in the Forth Valley, which now replaced southern Pictland as the focus of the Scottish kingdom. Following the example set by David I from the 1120s, many new burghs were created, usually with Roman-style rectilinear plans, such as that of Perth, laid out c. 1130. The plan might be modified to give priority to key monuments, as at St Andrews, where the three main streets were arranged to converge on the ecclesiastical precinct [18]. But these were nothing like the dense city-state towns of Italy and the Low Countries. They were more like large villages, with wooden houses [76], workshops and agricultural activity jumbled together on their long burgage plots [72], straggling back from the single main street. Only from the 14th century did towns like Perth see the building of stone houses on the street frontage. Scottish burghs generally had only one parish church (probably because

32 Roslin Collegiate Chapel, Midlothian, 1440s–60s: detail of the south end of the ambulatory, showing the flat lintels and the spiral-carved 'Apprentice Pillar'.

33 St Giles's Cathedral, Edinburgh, as it appeared in 1890 after successive 19th-century modernizations (for its earlier appearance, see ills. 72, 75). The 12th-century church and its later aisles were externally and internally unified, and shorn of numerous partitions and excrescences, by William Burn in 1829–33 and William Hay in 1871–83. The late 15th-century tower and crown spire, symbol of royal power, escaped the restorers' attentions.

most burghs and parishes were established at the same time, under David I), and thus these churches tended to spread crab-like, with numerous chantries and chapels. From the 15th century, and especially after the loss of Berwick to England in 1482, there was a growing centralization of activity in Edinburgh, which became the regular seat of parliament as well as a royal residence. The town church of St Giles's [33, 72, 75], originally a 12th-century Romanesque building, was progressively enlarged with additional ranges of aisles. In the late 15th century, it also acquired a tower topped by a crown steeple – a group of intersecting flying buttresses in the shape of a closed, or imperial, crown. The latter was a symbol understood across Europe of the new, untrammelled sovereignty claimed by kings within their realms, spelling the end of any idea of unified Christendom. In 1469 James III had claimed 'ful jurisdictioune and fre impire within his realme'. The building of the Edinburgh steeple shortly afterwards, along with others such as those of Linlithgow Church, West Lothian (c. 1480–90), and the chapel of King's College, Aberdeen, trumpeted in stone that new status. The crown steeples are a striking example of the way in which medieval architecture's symbolic requirements led to bold transpositions of scale – whether from jewelry to architecture, as here, or in the other direction, from buildings to spired reliquaries or canopied stalls.

The Birth of the Scottish Castle

Throughout Christendom, the Middle Ages saw the emergence of the castle as a symbol (again universally understood) of authority and faith, and, more particularly, as the practical focus for the ever more entrenched power of local magnates. Its functional requirements were a hall for feasting, some private sleeping accommodation, a kitchen and a chapel. The hall was the core of the accommodation, and increasingly developed into two variants, which might co-exist or overlap: a private laird's hall, often placed in a tower along with the other family accommodation, and a public great hall, often built separately as part of a horizontally disposed courtyard complex, not unlike a monastic cloister layout.

During the 12th and even the 13th century, the predominant pattern of castle in Scotland, as throughout north-west Europe, was the motte – an earthwork mound with a timber structure on top, sometimes surrounded by an enclosure with a separate hall. Some mottes were built adjacent to burghs, to reinforce the combination of lordly and judicial power. Others were sited in key rural locations, such as the 12th-century Doune of Invernochty in Strathdon, Aberdeenshire [34], one of the finest earthwork castles in Scotland, a motte 12 metres (40 feet) high sculpted out of a natural hill and originally topped by a timber hall and ringed by a water-filled moat, to form a stronghold of the Earldom of Mar.

34 Doune of Invernochty, Aberdeenshire: the 12th-century motte originally held a timber hall and was protected by a moat.

Some were built in several phases: at Courthill, Dalry, Ayrshire, a motte was built over the remains of a destroyed 12th-century timber-framed hall.

Some earthwork and timber castles continued to be built in the late Middle Ages. But from around the 11th century, especially in the Loire Valley and Norman England, a new pattern of stone-built castle had begun to spread, ultimately inspired by Roman fortifications and towers built in dressed ashlar: the tall, rectangular 'donjon' tower, set on a mound like a motte, and incorporating a hall above a vaulted basement, and private rooms above. During the 12th and early 13th centuries, various plan variations incorporating the donjon were tried, including circular or concentric layouts; Edward I's grand castles of occupation in Wales of the 1280s, such as Harlech, combined a quadrangular towered curtain wall and an inner block of lodgings. In Scotland, England and Spain, the prolonged periods of peace (in the Scottish case, both before and after the Wars of Independence) allowed

35 Bothwell Castle, Lanarkshire: on the left, closest to the bend in the river, are the remains of the late 13th-century donjon; extending inland is the courtyard complex, successively rebuilt, including a round corner tower in French style added as part of a major campaign after 1400.

36 Caerlaverock Castle, Dumfriesshire: the original triangular castle was built *c.* 1260–70, with two corner towers, a massive twin-towered gatehouse at the third corner (left), and a central courtyard. After 1637 a classical lodging block was inserted in the courtyard by the 1st Earl of Nithsdale.

the development of this donjon model into the 'show-castle' – a symbolic fusion of earthly aristocratic power and visionary Jerusalem.

In Scotland, the stone-built tower gained an almost unique symbolic status from a very early date. The first such castles were erected in the late 12th century, the earliest survivor today being Castle Sween in the West Highlands, which consists of a high stone wall with timber structures inside, not unlike a broch. During the 13th century, a wide variety developed, from the modest hall-house (with a hall raised on a vaulted undercroft), such as the mid-13th-century Skipness in Argyll, to complex courtyard groups. In contrast to occupied Wales, the most ambitious show-castles were freely begun by Scottish magnates, especially in the 13th century, prior to the Wars of Independence. Later, in the wake of King Robert the Bruce's scorched earth policy in the early 14th century, the pace of building quickened, as many destroyed earthwork castles were replaced in stone. Most of the greatest castles were multi-phase buildings spanning the entire period from the 13th to the 15th centuries. For example, at Bothwell, Lanarkshire [35], an ambitious late 13th-century project

for a massive circular donjon with an upper-level great hall and surrounded by an extensive courtyard complex was frustrated by repeated Scottish or English attacks; after 1362 the castle was consolidated on a reduced scale by Archibald the Grim, and then recast again after 1400; the curtain wall was strengthened, and a new hall, lodging block, chapel, and French-style round corner tower were built. Kildrummy Castle, Aberdeenshire, built just before 1300 for the Earl of Mar to replace the nearby Invernochty motte, was probably designed by an English royal mason, as suggested by its somewhat Harlech-like symmetrical curtain-walled plan, with a hall block inside the courtyard. An even more striking geometrical plan was devised by Aymer Maxwell, Chamberlain of Scotland, at his south-western castle of Caerlaverock, Dumfriesshire [36], built in dressed ashlar c. 1260–70: this takes the form of a precise triangle, with angle towers and gatehouse at the apex. And at Rothesay on the isle of Bute, a circular-plan castle, possibly superimposed on an existing motte, was built in the early 13th century by Walter, 3rd Steward of Scotland; after 1263, a gatehouse and four turrets were added.

For the medium-size castle, from the 14th century onwards the compact tower-house, or tower with hall range, became the norm: for example Smailholm, Roxburghshire [37], a small 15th-century tower-house, had a detached hall adjacent to it. In such

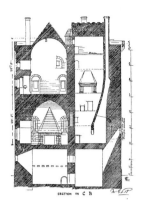

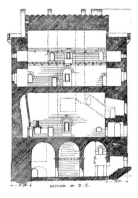

39, 40 Borthwick Castle, Midlothian, after 1430: transverse and longitudinal sections. The complex arrangements of rooms, flues, and stairs are clearly shown. Above the lowest level is the great hall with its pointed barrel vault; its massive hooded fireplace is seen end-on in the transverse section, and at the left end of the longitudinal section. (From David MacGibbon and Thomas Ross, *The Castellated and Domestic Architecture of Scotland*, 1, 1887)

modest yet imposing designs, the show-castle achieved an unparallelled breadth of social coverage. Only exceptionally was all accommodation contained within a single main block: at Hermitage in Liddesdale, Roxburghshire (a Douglas stronghold), between 1358 and 1400 a number of accretions to a rectangular tower created a symmetrical arrangement of wings unified by a huge pointed arch [38]. The predominance of the tower formula, coupled with a gradual rise in the standard of living and greater demands for privacy, led to a growing complexity of internal planning. At Borthwick Castle in Midlothian, built after 1430, the grandly severe castellated exterior conceals a warren of rooms on different levels [39, 40]. At the centre, reached by the only straight flight of stairs, is a church-like two-storey hall with pointed barrel vault and canopied fireplace; five spiral stairs link various other floors, creating segregated lodgings.

Palaces and forts: the onset of the Renaissance
In general, across Europe, the 15th and early 16th centuries were a time when domestic and religious architecture began to follow separate paths. In Scotland, as we have seen, there was a somewhat different tendency, towards the absorption of 'religious' by 'secular' architecture – although the construction of domestic architecture remained largely a matter of harled rubble, in contrast to the ashlar of the larger churches. By the mid-15th century, the strong Stewart monarchs, asserting their new 'imperial' status, were moving beyond the earlier magnates' domineering towers to a more subtle way of demonstrating power and prestige, informed by the new concepts of humanistic learning broadly known as the Renaissance. Architectural treatises and pattern books began to replace the practical geometry of the masons. Overtly military elements were increasingly hived off to a new discipline of scientific fortification, developed largely in Italy, while domestic architecture became more ornamental and refined, with castle features such as turrets and corbels reduced to a courtly veneer, and increasingly influenced by the new classical vocabulary.

The building of royal residences rather than castles had first emerged on a modest scale in the 1320s, when King Robert the Bruce built a country house with 'painted chambers' at Cardross, near Dumbarton. In the 1370s, Robert II (r. 1371–90) commissioned a major reconstruction of the war-damaged Stewart stronghold of Dundonald, Ayrshire, including a monumental four-storey square tower with two halls above one another,

41 Linlithgow, West Lothian: aerial view of the palace and St Michael's Parish Church. In the palace, the great hall, east entrance and forework are on the right of the courtyard, and the chapel at the front (cf. ill. 45). The church, begun c. 1480–90, originally had a crown spire; an aluminium evocation was added in 1964 by Geoffrey Clarke.

42 Linlithgow Palace: the east portal, probably after 1477. A coat of arms fits between the portcullis grooves; the niches have canopies topped by conventionalized images of Jerusalem.

43 Stirling Castle: the great hall, completed in 1503 by James IV. At the time this was the largest secular space in Scotland. The bay window lights the high-table end within. The structure (long used as barracks) was radically 'restored' in castellated style, as seen in this view, in 2000.

44 Falkland Palace, Fife: the north façade of the chapel block, facing the courtyard, as remodelled by James V after 1538. The regular classical detailing includes roundels containing portrait busts.

45 Linlithgow Palace, West Lothian: plan (cf. ill. 41). Although the courtyard plan was initially established in the 1420s during the reign of James I, the main features of the palace were completed subsequently. The south and west sides were largely built under James III; three of the four corner towers, the chapel, and the 'outer great façade', protruding from the east façade, by James IV. A new south gatehouse was begun in 1534 by James Hamilton of Finnart for James V. The north side of the courtyard was rebuilt by James VI & I from 1618 (ill. 68).

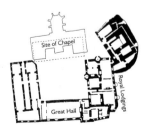

46 Edinburgh Castle: plan. The chief elements visible are James IV's great hall of c. 1500–1510; the royal lodgings, initially built by James IV in the same years and reconstructed by James VI & I in 1615–17; and (in outline at the top) the Scottish National War Memorial by R. S. Lorimer, of 1924–27 (ill. 176).

the upper hall having a pointed barrel vault with cross ribs (of the sort that was to appear in the 15th-century 'castle style' of church building). But it was only from the reign of James I (r. 1406–37) that palace building began in earnest, in some cases colonizing existing castles or monasteries. The basic formula was the same as for noblemen's large courtyard houses, except that the king and queen required separate lodgings, and everything was more lavishly decorated and on a larger scale, especially the great halls: the royal household comprised 300–350 people by the early 16th century. James I and his successors set out to emulate the opulent palaces of England and France, with a new emphasis on neo-chivalric display, including a cult of King Arthur and an artistic cosmopolitanism grounded in links with Italy and the Mediterranean: James IV (r. 1488–1513) had an especially expansionist outlook, symbolized by his construction in 1511 of the largest naval ship of the age, the 1,000-ton 'Michael'. James I began by building two completely new palaces, at Linlithgow (1424–28) and at Leith near Edinburgh (1434). The latter has now disappeared, but Linlithgow, which comprised a walled courtyard with a tall range of hall and lodgings on the east, was progressively expanded by James's successors into a unified quadrangular block, with a tower at each angle [41, 45], in the manner of Italian seigneurial palaces of the 15th century, as well as some recent houses in England. James III's friend Anselm Adornes became keeper of the palace in 1477, and the complex scheme of decoration above the east gateway [42], including symbolic images of Jerusalem, may have stemmed from his influence.

Between 1500 and his death in battle against the English in 1513, James IV made substantial contributions to all the other main royal palaces, including new lodging quarters and great halls at Edinburgh [46] and Stirling (the Stirling hall [43, 47], completed in 1503, was the largest secular space in Scotland) and a grand new turreted gatehouse forework at the latter. His successor, James V (r. 1513–42), at first continued the policy of chivalric turreted eclecticism, for example in a new donjon of lodgings at Holyrood (1528–32) [48, 61]. But there was, for a time, a radical change after 1537 when he married the eldest daughter of the King of France, François I, and then after her death Marie, daughter of the Duc de Guise. Six royal masons were sent from France, bringing with them the mainstream Renaissance practice of copying classical details based on the orders – Doric, Ionic and Corinthian – from pattern-books, and a new focus on the design of formal façades. From 1538 onwards, James remodelled the courtyard façades of

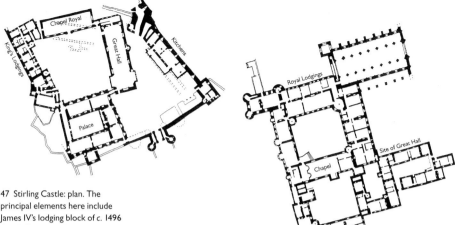

47 Stirling Castle: plan. The principal elements here include James IV's lodging block of c. 1496 (top left), great hall, completed in 1503, and turreted forework of c. 1500–1506 (at the centre of the south wall; later truncated); James V's quadrangular palace block of 1538–42; and the Chapel Royal, reconstructed from 1594 by William Schaw for James VI.

48 Holyrood Palace, Edinburgh: plan as it was in 1663 before the radical rebuilding in 1671–79 (ill. 61). The abbey church is at top right. The palace had been virtually rebuilt in quadrangular form by James IV in 1501–5. In 1528–32 James V added a tower of royal apartments (top left) and reconstructed the south and west ranges, including a new chapel in the former.

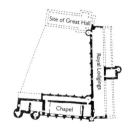

49 Falkland Palace, Fife: plan. James IV began the main buildings round the courtyard, including the chapel (completed 1512) and the twin-towered south-west gatehouse (completed 1541). The courtyard façades of the east and south quarters were reconstructed from 1538 by James V in a classical manner (ill. 44).

his country palace, Falkland in Fife [44, 49], with an orderly arrangement of pilasters and piers – an up-to-date style introduced to France less than thirty years previously. At Stirling, James added a new palace block in 1538–42 in a more unconventional classical style, composed of advanced and recessed wall-planes, with wide cusped arches framing statues on balusters and columns [50].

James V's new works at Falkland, Stirling and other palaces demonstrated the growing authority of a new, higher-status figure detached from the building trades: the 'royal master of work'. At Falkland this role was filled by James Scrymgeour of Myres, a heraldic expert, and at Stirling by James Hamilton of Finnart, an influential courtier until his execution for alleged treason in 1540. Finnart was also a prominent exponent of the new Renaissance imagery of fortification. He supervised the building of several royal forts in the 1530s, at Blackness in West Lothian and Tantallon in East Lothian, and laid out several show-fortifications, including gatehouses bristling with gun-ports at Linlithgow Palace (from 1534), and an unusual country mansion for himself at Craignethan, Lanarkshire, set inside a symmetrical artillery fortification, including the modish feature of a caponier (a covered firing gallery). By contrast with this Düreresque imagery, the reality of the new science of military design, with its geometrical angle bastions, was emphasized in a number of fortified 'blockhouses' built across southern Scotland under the francophile governorship of the Duke of Albany (1515–17 and 1521–24), under the guidance of Italian or French engineers: notable examples included Dunbar

50 Stirling Castle: the palace block
added by James V in 1538–42.
Between the windows, in an
idiosyncratic arrangement, are
cusped arches framing statues set
on tall ornamented bases.

(c. 1514–23) and St Andrews (from 1523). Italian fortress engineers may also have assisted in importing pattern-book classical detailing to the palaces and other civil building projects.

One of the key aspects of James IV's ethos of grandeur was the assertion of centralized power over the whole kingdom, through the forfeiture (abolition) in 1493 of the mighty Lordship of the Isles – an autonomous statelet, centred in Argyll and dominated by the MacDonald lords, that had largely inherited the mantle of Dál Riata. Architecturally, the peripatetic MacDonald lordship remained close to the early Christian pattern, avoiding the construction of grandiose buildings. Its main power centre was Finlaggan, on the island of Islay, where the Council of the Isles met on two islets in the middle of a loch, with inauguration-stones, a chapel and a great hall 18 metres (59 feet) long. All these buildings were demolished in 1494, and James IV, like Edward I in Wales, commenced a number of showpiece building projects to intimidate the local people; Rothesay Castle was enlarged in 1512–14 with a massive residential donjon. The cultural gap created by the forfeiture was partly filled by the MacLeods of Dunvegan, Skye, who built Rodel Church on the island of Harris in the early 16th century as a family burial place: it is a cruciform building with a broad western tower, and somewhat 'Irish' detailing similar to that of Iona Abbey, including a wheel-traceried chancel window.

Conclusion

By the time of the Reformation, from 1560, the precocious triumph of the show-castle, in parallel with the retrenchment of orthodox church Gothic, had laid the foundations for a more comprehensive secularization of Scottish architecture. It had also made possible an early and eclectic Scottish embrace of the Renaissance, characterized by a competition between castellar romanticism and pattern-book classicism – a tension that would endure for at least the next century.

51 George Heriot's Hospital,
Edinburgh, designed probably by
James Murray of Kilbaberton and
begun in 1628: view of the south
façade. The Gothic windows of the
chapel are contained within a
symmetrical classical arrangement.

Chapter 3   1560–1700: Age of Revolutions

The century and a half covered by this chapter was a time of constant strife, in both religious and secular affairs. The year 1560 saw the triumph in Scotland of the Reformation, a revolution which was carried through mainly by a landed oligarchy claiming to act in the interests of the 'commonalty of Scotland'. Calvinism, the branch of Protestantism which predominated in Scotland, fiercely rejected any authority of bishops and kings over the conscience of the individual Christian, and instead emphasized the role of an elected oligarchy of elders – whence the name 'Presbyterian' – and a religious liturgy dominated by the preaching of the Word rather than by masses and ceremonies. Over the rest of this period, that revolution was contested by rival Christian denominations, especially Anglican-style 'Episcopalianism' (so called because it gave authority to bishops). Presbyterianism finally triumphed only in 1689. Alongside these religious differences, there was also constant strife over dynastic and national affiliation. In 1603, James VI (who had assumed the crown in 1578) also became James I of England, and the court moved south – the first stage in the successively reinforced Protestant union of 'Great Britain'. But James and his successor, Charles I (r. 1625–49), both remained hostile to the Presbyterian ascendancy in Scotland, and fought to dilute it and to uphold the ideal of absolute monarchy. Eventually, from 1638 onwards, Charles's political and religious opponents in Scotland (the 'Covenanters') rose up against him, triggering a series of civil conflicts which drew in the remainder of Britain and Ireland, and involved Scotland in an English republican military occupation in the 1650s. That occupation was followed by a succession of royal régimes, with the absolutist Stuart 'Restoration' (Charles II, r. 1660–85, and James VII & II, r. 1685–89) in its turn overthrown in 1689 by a pro-Presbyterian faction, in the wake of the successful Dutch invasion of England. In general, each of these conflicts and settlements, especially following the union of the crowns in 1603, entangled Scotland more and more deeply in 'British' affairs, and increased the influence of England at the expense of France and Rome.

In this contest of dynasties and denominations, a central role was played by the Renaissance ideals of humanism and the new concern for the classical or the national past. All these could be used in justifying or condemning the concepts of imperial monarchy or 'republican' liberty. For building, the most immediate effect of these clashes was a new spell of interruption and destruction, not only by armies but by the three phases of Protestant iconoclasm (1560s, 1640s, late 1680s). And the English military occupation of the 1650s brought the construction of numerous garrison fortresses, complete with advanced polygonal plans and triangular bastions.

More fundamental changes were also under way, affecting the basic patterns of building types. We saw above that, although religious building had been central to Scottish society since prehistoric times, a gradual shift towards the secular had begun in the late Middle Ages. The victory of Calvinist Protestantism merely accentuated that trend. From 1603 onwards, under an absentee monarchy, the most important patrons became the landed classes, with their country houses and castles. Scotland was still an overwhelmingly rural country: even in the late 17th century, the largest town, Edinburgh, only had 30,000 inhabitants. For the lairds, in this time of flux, the concern was to stress their roots and their classical learning; yet they were also centrally involved in the first stages of the fostering of commerce and industry.

One consequence of this broadening in the social base of architecture was the increasing emergence of named architects, stemming from the landed class itself or from artisan origins. Although master masons still designed most buildings in the early 17th century, the most important design decisions in royal projects were made by the masters of work, such as William Schaw (in office 1583–1602) and James Murray (1607–34), rather than the royal master masons, such as William Wallace (d. 1631) and William Aytoun (d. c. 1643). Significantly, it was Schaw who now personally set about codifying the principles of modern freemasonry – a 'craft' that had nothing to do with actual building. By the late 17th century, the old type of mason was fading fast. The two dominant Scottish designers of this period, Sir William Bruce (c. 1630–1710) and James Smith (c. 1645–1731), illustrate alternative social contexts of architectural design. Bruce was a landowner, influential courtier and government official during the early years of the Stuart restoration, in the 1660s and 1670s. He flourished under the patronage of the powerful Earl of Lauderdale, the King's Commissioner (or viceroy) in Scotland. Charles II in 1671 appointed him 'surveyor general and overseer of the King's Buildings in Scotland'. His political fall in 1678 led to a loss of architectural office, and he was replaced as royal surveyor in 1683 by Smith, whereupon he retired to his country estate at Kinross to build his ideal classical house [70, 71]. The career of Smith, a lapsed Catholic who had spent time in Rome studying for the priesthood, began in a more humble way, as a mason and contractor. He became prominent in the 1680s and 1690s, and worked as a consultant designer on numerous large country houses and villas, only to ruin his fortunes by ill-judged coal-mining ventures.

Architecturally, just as in wider cultural terms, the Renaissance ideals of humanist learning became ever more pervasive, but there was a conflict about what they meant – especially in relation to the past. There was growing tension between the universal claims of classical antiquity and Scotland's own castle tradition: the royal projects and the masters of work tended to promote the former, while the landed classes and their masons remained more faithful to the latter. This classical-castellar tension is seen at its most extreme in George Heriot's Hospital in Edinburgh [51, 73], a palace-like college, designed probably by James Murray and built from 1628, with the help of the royal masons Wallace and Aytoun. This massive building combines classical symmetry and detailing with a turreted 'medieval' skyline (complete with bartizans, or projecting angle turrets) and Gothic chapel windows.

But we must guard against anachronism: this was not some Battle of the Styles in the 19th-century sense, fuelled by accurate 'archaeological' source-books (such as R. W. Billings' *Antiquities* [31]) and other modern publications. In fact, there is, at present, almost no documentary evidence of the views of 16th- and early 17th-century patrons and designers, and it seems likely that each building had its own particular recipe of elements. Only from the 1670s, under Bruce and Smith, was there a decisive shift towards classicism as a system of values, integrating appearance, plan and purpose, and epitomized by the orders, with their connotations of ideal Platonic forms and a wider universal harmony. Even then, in contrast to precise 19th-century styles, there was no one 'correct' classicism or single concept of the 'national': poor communications and imperfect archaeological knowledge insured there were innumerable local variations.

Post-Reformation churches

Scottish church architecture since 1560 has passed through periods of inactivity and others of enthusiastic building. The time immediately following the Reformation was the least active of all, as the doctrines of Calvinism, with their emphasis on preaching, left the country's stock of religious houses largely redundant, and its churches stripped of altars and ornament. All that was required now in a parish church was a modest preaching hall, and there was usually no question of any new construction, other than sometimes the addition of a separate wing (known in Scotland as an aisle) with accommodation for the local laird, making a T-shaped layout. The secular world also fed off the old religious building stock: as the extensive complexes of halls, lodgings and cloisters at places such as Arbroath Abbey became redundant, they were used as quarries of building stone by the expanding burghs. Although the years up to 1690 saw a see-sawing of fortunes between Presbyterian and Episcopal interpretations of reformed worship, there was never sufficient opportunity or need for either faction to build on a large scale, and thus it is impossible to make generalizations about architectural style.

Some stylistic connotations or associations can, however, be guessed at from a handful of model churches built during the period by the competing factions. Little is known about Scotland's first post-Reformation church, at Forfar in Angus (1564): a map prepared between 1585 and 1596 shows a structure with a central tower and three wings. The earliest surviving Presbyterian church is St Columba's, Burntisland, Fife [52, 53], built from 1589 by an alliance between the kirk elders and prominent local merchants, with John Roche as mason. It has a unique centralized design, with a tower (originally crowned by a wooden steeple) supported internally on four great arches, and surrounding aisles under a pyramidal roof. The squat, square building is neither Gothic nor classical, but essentially a local response to the preaching-orientated requirements of Reformed worship.

Five years later, the young James VI, beginning to seek ways to curb the Presbyterians, commissioned Schaw to design a new Chapel Royal at Stirling Castle for the christening of his son. The resulting building, while essentially still a simple rectangular box for Presbyterian worship, externally recalls a Florentine palazzo in its round-arched refinement and its scholarly classical doorcase.

52, 53 St Columba's Parish Church, Burntisland, Fife, begun in 1589: views of the exterior and of the interior, where the centralized preaching-space below the tower is ringed by aisles filled with seating.

54 Canongate Parish Church, Edinburgh, by James Smith, 1688. Calton Hill is seen in the background of this early 20th-century view. The Roman Doric theme established in the front portico is continued inside in the supporting columns of the round-arched arcade.

By 1621, the royal campaign to revive Episcopalian ceremony had made further gains, and James's ally, Archbishop Spottiswoode of St Andrews, felt confident enough to build a model church at Dairsie in Fife 'after the English form', for Anglican-style worship. The plan revived the east–west linearity of the Middle Ages, and the plate-traceried Gothic windows and octagonal spire further suggested a continuity with the medieval church. Unsurprisingly, the building was sacked by iconoclasts in the 1640s. The final model church of this intermittent and ultimately unsuccessful campaign against the Presbyterians was built in the 1680s, after James VII & II decided to make Holyrood Abbey Kirk the home of his revived Order of the Thistle. To house the displaced congregation of this part of Edinburgh, James Smith designed a new Canongate Parish Church in 1688 [54], combining a Presbyterian preaching-box interior with hints of contemporary Catholic church architecture, including a Latin-cross plan and a broad, curved front gable.

Great Houses and Palaces: the Rise of the 'Stately Home'
In the mid-16th century, the great castles of the Scottish landed classes still combined not only living, cooking and sleeping accommodation but also government and justice quarters. But already, as we saw above, the rise in living standards and the

spread of the Renaissance ideal of order was changing all that, by requiring increased privacy and space, while presenting a more stately image to the outside world. Eventually, in the 19th century, Scotland would be one of the leading countries in spreading this new domestic order across most of society; but for the moment its benefits were confined to a narrow élite.

The architectural expression of this process changed markedly in the course of the 17th century. In the years from 1560 until around 1660 or 1670, there was a sharp division between the interior of houses, their landscape setting, and their exterior design. Inside, despite the retention of massive stone construction, planning became more rational, and quite unlike the jumbled-together arrangements of the 12th and 13th centuries. To accommodate both family privacy and large numbers of guests, the old stack of single chambers was replaced by coordinated groups of spaces, strung together both horizontally and vertically. Many Continental palace layouts by the mid-16th century comprised symmetrical, cellular agglomerations of 'apartments' – autonomous suites of rooms centred around a principal sequence of reception chamber, antechamber and bedroom. In Renaissance Italy, these rooms were arranged ideally in line, or in clustered or spiral plans if space was limited. The latter was usually the case in Scotland [65]. The old raised main floor became a kind of piano nobile, and into the confined space of the castle were shoehorned the new apartment sequences, arranged in increasing order of intimacy, from outer hall to bedchamber, served by the same complex networks of staircases as before (the formal public stair rose in a straight flight to the first floor, and separate turnpike stairs carried on to the private floors beyond). Interiors up to the early 17th century remained faithful to tapestry-hung walls and painted ceilings, but, beginning with the 1617 royal palace block at Edinburgh Castle, a fashion came in for white plaster ceilings divided up into geometrical compartments.

The landscape setting of houses in these years also became more straightforwardly classical. It conformed to the Europe-wide pattern of the formal Renaissance garden, with its statues, fountains, terraces and arbours, and its symbolic cosmological layouts inspired by contemporary Humanist philosophy. In Scotland this was often surrounded by high walls, as at Edzell Castle in Angus [55], where a garden was laid out in 1604 by the mining and forestry magnate Sir David Lindsay, its walls ornamented with Dürer-style carved representations of the Planetary Deities, Liberal Arts and Cardinal Virtues.

55 Edzell Castle, Angus: aerial view. The original tower-house (overlooking the garden) was built in the early 16th century. It was extended c. 1542 with a gatehouse and hall range (immediately behind it in this view), and an even larger and grander hall range was added at right angles (top right) in the late 16th century, forming a courtyard group. The geometrical garden of 1604 is surrounded by an elaborately decorated and pavilioned wall.

The country house exterior was a different story. Here the now entrenched image of the Scottish castle continued to reign supreme until the 1660s. Usually, owing to the solidity of their stone construction, great houses were built by accretion rather than from new, and were surrounded by temporary service buildings of turf or wood. To symbolize their venerable status, houses were often decorated with a profusion of theatrical castellar devices, including bartizans, gatehouses and armorial sculpture, and were crowned by viewing platforms [59]. Many incorporated classical details, even entire façades, but with very few exceptions these features were subordinate elements within an irregular, castle-like whole.

From the 1670s onwards, this all changed: the inside and outside of buildings and the landscaping became integrated within a single ethos of classical order [70]. There was a systematic move towards more segregated and stately plans, linked to a symmetrical classicism on the exterior [71]. The earlier hybrid apartments were replaced by more monumental, separate sequences of rooms for private or family use and for public display (the so-called state apartment or great apartment). Although some houses by Bruce introduced unprecedented standards of 'antique' gravity, most important projects were still for the rebuilding and 'reform' (remodelling) rather than complete replacement of castellated houses. Now, however, there was the challenging task of disguising this on the outside, squeezing in the monumental sequences of great apartments, and inserting early mod. cons. The latter ranged from water-closets to the new counterbalanced sash windows – invented in the English Royal Office of Works in 1669 and introduced by Scottish courtiers in the mid-1670s. The late 17th century was also the heyday of axial landscaping in the Versailles manner, which projected grandeur out into the landscape through radiating avenues and plantations, ultimately leaving the house a tiny speck in a vast ordered expanse.

The Last Castles: from Reassertion to Reform
It is possible to detect a very broad chronological development, with a mainstream of castellated architecture built by aristocrats, offset by the repeated challenges of classicism stemming from the royal court. The lack of evidence about the intentions of builders

56 Huntly Castle, Aberdeenshire. This early 19th-century view by James Giles shows the main block of the old House of Strathbogie (probably of early 15th-century origin) on the right, and the round tower of c. 1553 added by the 4th Earl of Huntly on the left. The castle was further reconstructed c. 1599–1606 by George Gordoun, 1st Marquess of Huntly, whose marriage to Lady Henrietta Stewart was commemorated in the grand inscription stretching across the oriel-windowed upper part of the façade.

57 Craigievar Castle, Aberdeenshire: the hall, with its lavish early 17th-century plasterwork.

58 Craigievar: section showing the superimposed lodgings, linking staircases and ceiling flues.

59 Craigievar: the original 16th-century tower was rebuilt after 1610 by William Forbes, who added a new corbelled and turreted superstructure for 'show', topped by two viewing platforms.

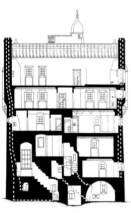

and designers makes it difficult to classify specific stylistic tendencies, however, and the problem is accentuated by imprecise terminology. A number of terms were in use: one list of country seats in 1570 talks of 'castellis, palices, houssis and places'. But these words overlapped considerably: 'palace' and 'place' generally referred to houses around courtyards, while during the late 16th and 17th centuries 'castle' became the preferred term for the most prestigious castellated houses, whether towered or with courtyards. In the more compact, vertically planned houses, derived from the older tower format, the demands for greater segregation and stateliness were more difficult to meet than in the horizontal 'palace' pattern.

The regency of James V's widow Mary of Guise (from 1554) and the subsequent period of active rule of her daughter Mary ('Queen of Scots' 1542–87) had already witnessed a renewed fashion for the show-castle, possibly forming part of a nostalgic Francophile fashion, harking back to the French châteaux of earlier days. A number of influential projects featured round towers in the style of a donjon. In the north-east, for instance, around 1553, George Gordoun, 4th Earl of Huntly, rebuilt the House of Strathbogie and changed its name to Huntly Castle: the existing castellar main block was augmented with a six-storey round tower of bedrooms [56]. And at Balvenie House, also in the north-east, the 4th Earl of Atholl prepared for a visit by Mary of Guise in 1556 by building a new palace block with a round corner tower. One outcome of this new fashion was the familiar late 16th-century Z-plan house, with a main block flanked by round angle towers, as at Claypotts Castle near Dundee, started in 1569 by John Strachan. The late 16th-century houses saw a gradual trend from round to square angle towers. In towns, although most great houses took the form of courtyard palaces, there also existed numbers of urban tower-houses – a pattern which overlapped with the civic wardhouse or tolbooth (town-house or municipal building) tower [78]. In the small rural town of Fordyce in Banffshire, an L-plan tower-house built in 1592 by Thomas Menzies of Aberdeen was surrounded by rows of single-storey houses, probably of timber, wattle and thatch at first, but later rebuilt in stone.

The most noteworthy group of late 16th- and early 17th-century tall towers was created in the north-east, and was associated with two contrasting phases of patronage and style. At first, during a local resurgence of Catholicism in the 1570s–90s, towers were built which combined an external austerity with

'medievalizing' internal features such as groin vaults. Then followed a series of projects by Protestant lairds in the early 17th century, many designed by the Bel family of masons, with exuberant external decoration and internal plasterwork. The most dramatic example is Craigievar, Aberdeenshire [57–59], where a 'Catholic' tower with vaulted great hall was heightened and lavishly ornamented after 1610 by a Protestant merchant, William Forbes. Again in the north-east, in the same years, prior to 1617, Ian Bel completed Muchall – renamed Castle Fraser at that time – with a showy reconstruction of the upper storeys with corbelled turrets and huge north-facing coat of arms; a large pre-existing round tower was capped by a balustraded viewing platform.

The 'palace' formula, planned around a courtyard, made the arrangement of rooms in imposing apartment sequences much easier. In Denmark, England and elsewhere in Northern Europe, the years around 1600 saw the construction of various show-palaces with regular, symmetrical plans and turreted, castle-like skylines. Scottish country houses were mostly expanded more modestly from existing towers through the addition of a laird's lodging block; one side of a courtyard was often taken up with a gallery, usually overlooking a view. Yet again in the north-east, for example, William Forbes of Tolquhon in 1584–89 refashioned his

60 Fyvie Castle, Aberdeenshire, as enlarged after 1596: the new main façade with its 'triumphal arch' centrepiece.

house into a compact courtyard group comprising a 'house, tower and place' – the 'tower' being the original castle, the 'house' being a four-storey lodging linked to the tower, and the 'place' being the courtyard as a whole, entered by a stumpy twin-towered gatehouse. Palace courtyards did not have to be completely enclosed. Dudhope Castle, situated in a commanding position overlooking the burgh of Dundee, was built from c. 1580 by a local laird, and comprises two wings at an irregular angle, with round towers at the corners and ends and flanking the main entrance. As with tower-houses, the late 16th-century palaces saw a trend from round to square angle towers. At Hamilton Palace in Lanarkshire, completed by 1595, the main façade had flanking four-storey rectangular towers and ornamental chimneys, and at Fyvie Castle in the north-east, enlarged by the chief government treasurer Alexander Seton from 1596, an impressively showy garden façade was added to an existing palace group, with flanking square towers and a twin-towered centrepiece in the style of a Roman triumphal archway [60].

After the interruption of the period of war and occupation in the 1640s and 1650s, the desire to enhance and rebuild castle-like courtyard palaces was given a boost by the Restoration emphasis on revived tradition and lineage. New houses in this style were almost out of the question – although Patrick Smyth of Braco built a virtually new quadrangular 'castle' at Methven, near Perth, around 1678, possibly to the designs of James Smith. The grandly sited building, retaining some earlier fabric internally, has a round turret at each corner, anticipating the revived castles of the 18th century. At first, the predominant approach was to retain but remodel the old houses along lines of greater order, symmetry and internal grandeur. The general principles of this respectful 'reform' were adumbrated in the royal reconstruction of Holyrood Palace, or Holyroodhouse, in 1671–79 [61]. The project was designed by Bruce, with Smith acting as master mason, working to the instructions of the Earl of Lauderdale. Here, the practical requirement for the revived absolutist monarchy of Charles II was to provide accommodation for Lauderdale and visiting royals, and working apartments for the officers of state and the privy council. James V's great tower was retained and converted into one wing of a symmetrical composition, by building a matching replica to the south, linked by a range with a central entrance flanked by coupled giant columns, and with a plainer classical courtyard behind. Inside, a grand stone staircase on one side gives access to separate king's and queen's great apartments,

61 Holyrood Palace, Edinburgh: aerial view of the palace as reconstructed in 1671–79 to the designs of Sir William Bruce. The 16th-century lodging tower is on the left, and the new, matching south tower on the right. Between them and behind is Bruce's symmetrical classical courtyard arrangement. (The ruined medieval abbey church appears top left. It had been sacked by a Protestant mob in 1688, and the roof collapsed in 1768.)

62 Glamis Castle, Angus, rebuilt in near-symmetrical though un-classical fashion in 1670–79 by the 3rd Earl of Kinghorne in an effort to 'reduce the place to … uniformitie'. It was surrounded by a scheme of great axial avenues.

63 Thirlestane Castle, Lauder, as rebuilt by Sir William Bruce in 1670–77 ('Baronialized' after 1840 with high roofs and flanking blocks by William Burn and David Bryce).

and to the new privy council meeting hall in the south tower; a gallery is lined with royal portraits.

Key members of the Restoration régime set about reconstructing their towers in a similar way. In 1668–74, Bruce extended his own house, Balcaskie in Fife, transforming the vertical tower into a symmetrical, spreading range, with a matching tower at the other end, and big chimneys, gables and viewing platform in between. At Glamis Castle, Angus [62], in 1670–79, the 3rd Earl of Kinghorne, an ally of Lauderdale, tried to create a symmetrical composition out of a tower-house set at a diagonal angle by adding forward-thrusting wings flanking the turreted central mass. At Thirlestane in the Borders [63], Lauderdale's own seat, Bruce contrived an equally unconventional arrangement in 1670–77, with a symmetrical array of towers crowded at the entrance end of the elongated tower range. More usually, towers were incorporated in restful rectangular courtyard groups, following the Holyrood precedent. Drumlanrig Castle, Dumfriesshire, was the seat of the 1st Duke of Queensberry, a key courtier in the 1680s; James Smith's reconstruction in 1679–90 accentuated the spirit of an existing informal early 17th-century courtyard plan, and turned the house into a symmetrical four-

64 Drumlanrig Castle, remodelled by James Smith in 1679–90: the entrance façade.

65 Crichton Castle, Midlothian: plan of the principal (first) floor. The scale-and-platt staircase is at the west (left) end of the new north lodging range. The original tower house, on the east (in black), had been extended in the mid-15th century into a courtyard group formed by the hall on the south side and chambers on the west.

66 Crichton Castle: the new north lodging block built in the 1580s, with its arcade, scale-and-platt staircase and diamond rustication.

towered block like Heriot's Hospital [51] in overall profile, but with scholarly classical detail including a giant order on the entrance façade [64]. The gallery, above the main entrance, commands a vista of formal terraced gardens.

Court Architecture and the Classical Ideal

By the end of the 17th century, these regularized castellar houses were superseded by a more comprehensive classical approach. The antecedents of that outlook went back to the reign of James VI & I in the late 16th–early 17th century, which saw the rise of a new class of patrons, exemplified by Alexander Seton of Fyvie – professional courtiers rather than great nobles. Appealing to antiquity to bolster their prestige, they constructed a Roman ideal of the statesmanlike simple life. This led to a growing requirement for rural or suburban houses, villa-like in size, often incorporating ostentatious classical elements within an irregular, castellar framework, just like the royal palace extensions of the early 16th century. As early as the 1580s, the renegade but cosmopolitan Earl of Bothwell recast the north side of his courtyard castle of Crichton, south-east of Edinburgh, by building a new lodging block with a three-storey scale-and-platt (straight) staircase and a loggia to the courtyard with diamond rusticated walling above [65, 66].

From the 1590s, the courtier-like status of William Schaw and his successors, and the influence of the new Danish architectural ideas which arrived with James's queen, Anne of Denmark, encouraged a more rapid though still piecemeal spread of classicism.

For the first time since the early 16th century, a classical style of domestic architecture began to spread, heavily intermingled with castellar elements. This trend was especially associated, after 1603, with the building projects of prominent courtiers of the King and Queen, in the south-east of Scotland and just over the English border. George Home, Lord Berwick and Earl of Dunbar, commissioned James Murray in 1607 to design an ambitious mansion for him at Berwick on Tweed, symbolically overlooking the old border. The house, which was left unfinished at Home's death in 1611, had a flat roof and regular mullion-and-transomed fenestration. Its small flanking square towers gave it a continuing foothold in the castle world, and an affinity to English late Elizabethan houses such as Hardwick Hall. Another royal supporter, the mining magnate Edward, Lord Bruce of Kinloss, in 1608 began construction of Culross Abbey House in Fife, a two-storey, uniformly windowed classical block with ashlar facing and flanking square towers.

From the mid-1610s, a more thoroughly hybrid classical/castellar approach was developed in a number of new and enlarged houses and villas designed or influenced by James Murray. Unlike Inigo Jones, his English counterpart as royal architect, Murray had an evolutionary rather than revolutionary approach.

67 Linlithgow Palace, West Lothian: the courtyard, showing the north quarter, built by James Murray from 1618; on the right is the east entrance, after 1477. The transitional Gothic-classical King's Fountain was added in the early 16th century by James V.

68 Winton House, East Lothian, enlarged by James Murray in 1620–27: the drawing room, with its heraldic-decorated ceiling plasterwork and wide stone Roman Doric fireplace, seen in a late 19th-century photograph.

Building on the quadrangular towered palace tradition of Scotland and Denmark, he designed tall, symmetrical ranges with raised stair-towers and detail culled from French, Italian and Flemish pattern-books, such as buckle quoins [73] and strapwork finials. First, and most prestigious, were blocks of lodgings added to the royal palaces at Edinburgh (1615–17) and Linlithgow (from 1618). At the latter, the north courtyard façade [67] was sumptuously faced in ashlar, symmetrically arranged around an octagonal stair-tower, and adorned with pediments over the windows and classicizing ashlar chimneys. In various smaller houses in the Forth Valley in the 1620s and 1630s, mostly by Murray or his successor, Sir Anthony Alexander (d. 1637), we find balanced, rather than strictly symmetrical, U-plans with angle staircase towers, and a somewhat castle-like gabled verticality. These include Murray's own house, Kilbaberton, near Edinburgh (1623), Winton in East Lothian (1620–27), and Pitreavie in Fife (1630). Winton was built by the mining magnate Lord Seton around an old tower, with ashlar facing and lavish internal heraldic decoration, plasterwork and classical fireplaces [68]. A larger version of the same villa type was created c. 1620–23 by the master of Queen Anne's household, Sir Henry Lindsay of Kinfauns, at Careston, Angus, originally constructed c. 1586 and now remodelled, including grand armorial chimneypieces.

After the 1660s and 1670s, the growing preference for wholesale reconstruction led to a pressure for more unambiguously grand, horizontally proportioned classical gestures. The most monumental of these was commissioned from

69 Hamilton Palace, Lanarkshire, as enlarged by James Smith from 1684 onwards: the south front.

70 Kinross House, by Sir William Bruce, 1679–93: elevation, and plans of house and site. The drawings, showing the 'double depth' plan of the house and the vast, axial landscaping scheme, were probably made by the Episcopalian clergyman/designer Alexander Edward.

71 Kinross House: the garden façade. Note the rusticated basement, the giant order of pilasters above, and the attic windows set between the boldly projecting cornice and the eaves of the tall roof.

James Smith in 1684 by the 3rd Duke and Duchess of Hamilton, the foremost aristocrats of Scotland. Smith's design made no attempt to improve the old courtyard castle of Hamilton in the Holyrood manner, but simply planted a new U-plan classical frontage in front of it [69]. At its centre was the unprecedented feature of a giant tetrastyle Corinthian portico. Underlining the new emphasis on show, the west wing, containing the state apartment, was completed first, in 1693. A vast, Versailles-like axial landscaping scheme was laid out to north and south of the house in the 1690s. A similar but more modest remodelling was carried out in 1702–5 by Smith for Anne, Duchess of Buccleuch, at Dalkeith Palace in Midlothian by hollowing a U-shaped front courtyard out of the existing tower-house complex. The new sash-windowed, porticoed façade commanded a vast, axial landscape prospect.

The stage had now been reached where new classical houses almost free of references to castles could be built, and it was Bruce in the 1670s and 1680s who set out to do so – although both he and Smith were perfectly capable of working in both idioms. In two smaller houses of the late 1670s, Dunkeld and Moncrieffe, both in Perthshire, Bruce adumbrated a compact, villa-like plan-type with central salon and flanking main rooms; Dunkeld, in a residual link with the past, had small corner bartizans. For these smaller houses, English influences seemed to have been decisive: some were referred to not just as 'of the modern fashion' but 'after the English Modell'. It was only in a more ambitious project, for Bruce's own house, Kinross [70, 71], built gradually in 1679–93 in the years of his political eclipse, that he was able to make a complete break with the past. Rather than stretching out a single-depth great-apartment sequence, Bruce

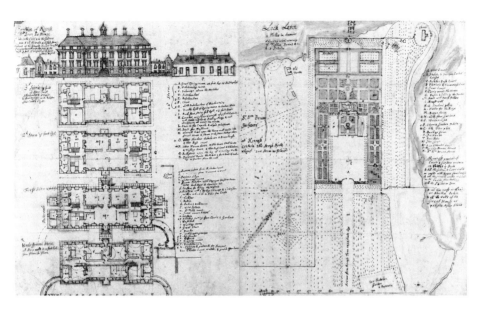

gave Kinross a more practical layout, two rooms deep with a double-height salon at the centre. Externally, the house conveys the small-windowed antique grandeur of a palazzo, entirely faced in finely finished ashlar. In a foretaste of the ideas of a century later, the castle heritage is now turned into a part of the designed landscape: the vista from Kinross's garden front is focused on the ruins of Lochleven Castle, within which Queen Mary had been imprisoned a century earlier; doubtless the motive was a desire to celebrate Stuart and Jacobite values. In later projects, such as Hopetoun House in West Lothian, Bruce was able to develop this new, uncompromising classicism: the first phase of Hopetoun, from 1698, was a relatively simple block with an octagonal staircase hall, but in 1702 rustication and angle pavilions were added, creating an image rather like a great French hôtel.

James Smith, too, was emboldened to begin building in a more assertively antique style, from the 1690s. At Melville House, Fife, of 1697–1702, the grand public rooms were encased in a relatively plain exterior, with rectangular corner towers in a residual trace of the castle tradition. However, a succession of more daring unbuilt proposals by Smith envisaged centralized or palazzo-like houses with three-storey porticoes or loggias. At his hands, the classical house also began to spread down the social scale, in the form of a new type of small villa, only one room deep, but still providing a degree of segregation of private and public: the pioneer was a house for himself at Whitehill, near Edinburgh, begun in 1686, which included a great apartment squeezed into the first floor, with an ingenious spiral layout.

Urban and Civic Architecture

This new, compact classical planning was also gradually applied to houses in towns. Earlier in the century, the largest were like small courtyard-plan castles, and began to break away from the traditional kind of urban tower-house towards a more symmetrical, classical pattern. At Argyll Lodging in Stirling, a tower was enlarged in 1632 into a U-plan courtyard block in the Kilbaberton manner, probably by Sir Anthony Alexander. (It was further enlarged in 1674.) Lower down the social scale, the growing burgh populations, during the 17th century, began to necessitate vertical and horizontal subdivision of sites, with the strip-like burgage plots increasingly filled with back buildings, and the street frontages built up higher and higher. On these frontages, the timber, wattle and thatch construction of the 16th century [76] was largely replaced by stone facing during the 17th century. In

Edinburgh [72, 76], purpose-built blocks of flats became the only way of building spacious dwellings in the urban core – a development, similar to that in Continental cities, that began to take Scotland and England further away from each other in their urban housing patterns.

The growing pressure on land in Edinburgh reflected its undisputed status, by the 1560s, as Scotland's 'capitall toune', a pressure first answered by the extension of existing buildings. In 1561–62, Queen Mary added a new tolbooth to the existing complex by St Giles's Kirk [72], and later in the century the church was subdivided to provide Reformed worship spaces and other utility rooms. But by the 17th century, the climate was right for rather larger projects, and the traditional building types of palace, hall and church began to be adapted for communal civic purposes. There was also a new awareness, influenced generally by antiquity and by humanist philosophy, of the image of the town or city as a whole; and there was the beginning of a desire to shape it in something other than a mere ad-hoc muddle – for example, by putting key public buildings in a geometrical relationship to each other. For absolutist rulers across Europe, the original inspiration

72 The High Street, Edinburgh: detail from Gordon of Rothiemay's perspective, 1647. In the centre is St Giles's (cf. ills 33, 75), with the tolbooth buildings immediately behind it. In front is the new L-plan Parliament House and Law Courts by James Murray, 1632–38. The drawing clearly shows the cramped layout of the medieval burgage plots at right angles to the street, stretching down to the Cowgate in the foreground. This congested area was radically thinned out during the 'improvements' of the mid- and late 19th century.

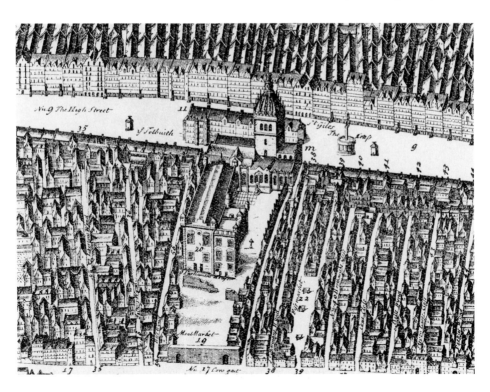

for these ideas was the city of Rome, later reinforced by the Versailles of Louis XIV.

A modest initial version of this vision was first conceived for Edinburgh under Charles I, as part of his strategy of curbing the Presbyterians. It included the conversion of St Giles's Kirk into an Episcopal cathedral and the construction of a new Parliament House and Law Courts next to St Giles's [72, 75]. Also built as part of this civic improvement drive was the quadrangular George Heriot's Hospital, a philanthropic school foundation on a palatial scale [51, 73]. It was begun in 1628, and the upper storeys, including the corner towers, were completed in the 1630s; the main belfry tower was only finished in 1693. The overall design and much of the detail (including the strapwork and the hall door) was culled from Italian or French pattern books.

That spiky, semi-medieval pattern was left behind in the project, designed by James Murray and built from 1632, for a new

73 George Heriot's Hospital, Edinburgh, designed probably by James Murray and begun in 1628: detail of the entrance archway. It is encrusted with detailing drawn from pattern-books: not only 'structural' elements such as the columns and voussoirs, but also a profusion of decorative embellishments covering most surfaces, including curly strapwork pediments, obelisk finials, rustication, and 'buckle quoins' at the angles of the building, which are especially characteristic of Murray's work.

74 Parliament House, Edinburgh, 1632–38: view of the main interior, with its original arched timber ceiling, probably designed by James Murray. This photograph, taken in 1893, shows the hall in its modern use as the central meeting space of the Scottish supreme law courts. In its original use, it was the home of the legislature: seating was arranged in a U around the timber throne of the King's High Commissioner, with the three or at times four 'estates' arranged in distinct blocks; the rest of the hall was occupied by movable seating for the law courts.

Parliament House adjacent to St Giles's [72. 75]. Though it might appear democratic, this was another exercise in royal absolutism, as the Scottish Parliament in the early 17th century was largely under the King's influence. A purpose-built parliament building was slightly unusual in 17th-century Europe, and its novelty was emphasized by its horizontal proportions and its almost flat roof – a marked departure from the high-roofed great hall tradition. The building was tied into the grouping of buildings around St Giles's by its concave-fronted L-plan, with the main hall running north-south, and a vaulted hall below. Externally, as one might expect in a design by the court architect, there was regular fenestration and profuse classical and strapwork decoration, combined with square bartizans at the corners. Internally, the flat roof is supported by a spectacular open timber ceiling [74], probably designed by Murray and still surviving today, comprising polygonal arches with radial members. Ironically, Parliament House was only completed in August 1638, by which time the revolution against royal power was under way, and the new building immediately became a redoubt of the Covenanters. Only in 1661, with the restoration of the monarchy, was the full royal parliamentary pomp instituted in the new legislature.

More generally, under the rule of Charles II and James VII & II the campaign of reshaping of Edinburgh was resumed – especially during James's period of personal residence at Holyrood, as Duke of Albany and York, in 1679–82. Under the Stuarts' relatively decentralized conception of the union, efforts were made to establish the capital of Scotland as a distinct focus of power and ceremony within Britain. Bruce's remodelling of Holyrood Palace in the 1670s [61] inspired a variety of aristocratic mansion-building projects in the Canongate. The most important was Queensberry House, begun in 1679 for the brother of the Duke of Lauderdale, and subsequently enlarged in the 1690s into a grand U-plan house by the 1st and 2nd Dukes of Queensberry, with modish slated roof and viewing platform. In the centre of Edinburgh, a devastating fire in 1676 brought opportunity for civic-sponsored renewal. Parliament Close was rearranged as a classical square, mainly by Thomas Robertson, a pioneering speculative builder, working with Bruce, Smith and Robert Mylne (1633–1710), the king's master mason. On the east side of the square, a new Merchants' Exchange, with an arched, colonnaded courtyard, was built in 1680–82 by Robertson, to the designs of Bruce and Smith. It only lasted for twenty years before another great fire in 1700. In 1685, the new status of Parliament Square as a Capitoline *place royale* was confirmed when an equestrian statue of King Charles II

75 Parliament Square, Edinburgh: a painting of 1844 (based on a late 18th-century prototype) evokes its appearance in the 1790s. The crowded space immediately south of St Giles's, with Parliament House on the left, is shown in exaggeratedly spacious form (cf. ill. 72), surrounding the statue of Charles II erected in 1685.

in the manner of Marcus Aurelius was erected, with classical dress and laurel wreath [75].

The main obstacle to the establishment of Edinburgh as a stately capital city was its tightly confined, rocky situation [72]. To provide fashionable dwellings with apartments of rooms, it would be necessary not only to build flats but to cut across the dense lines of burgage plots – producing a hybrid between private and public space. The late 17th century saw the first residential redevelopment schemes of tall courtyard-type blocks, including Milne's Square (1684–88) and Milne's Court (from 1695) [76]. It was James VII & II who suggested the logical next step in the escape from the rock: to build an extension to north or south, linked with the town by a bridge. This plan would only be realized in the next time of peace and prosperity, in the later 18th century.

Outside Edinburgh, the pressures of urban growth were less intense, and public building projects were smaller in scale. Most efforts were focused on the enlargement of tolbooths as centres of administration of the growing demands of burgh life. These buildings were like small castles, containing a vaulted prison and civic meeting-room above, with a squat attached steeple housing the all-important municipal clock. Prominent examples were the

76 Milne's Court, Edinburgh, by Robert Mylne, begun in 1695. In this mid-19th-century view it is still neighboured by timber-framed tenements typical of the late medieval High Street (cf. ill. 72). Prior to the 17th century, the architectural difference between Scottish towns and their contemporaries in other countries was far less pronounced: by the 19th century, the street façades of urban housing elsewhere in Northern Europe were dominated by plaster or brick.

77 Glasgow College, begun in 1630: a late 19th-century view showing the High Street façade and the steeple rising from the courtyards behind.

Aberdeen 'wardhouse' of 1616–30, and the Glasgow Tolbooth of 1625–27, with its slender steeple capped by a crown spire. Glasgow was by now rapidly emerging as a significant urban centre, and one of the largest public buildings of the age was developed there from 1630: Glasgow College, a university complex comprising two courtyards with tall steeple and classical street façade [77]. The tolbooth tradition of urban steeples continued into the 18th century in remoter locations – for example in the castle-like tower of Tain Tolbooth, Easter Ross [78], built in 1706–8 by master mason Alexander Stronach. And it also spread its influence abroad, in the scheme by the Scots engineer Christopher Galloway to heighten the imperial gate to the Moscow Kremlin, the Spassky or St Saviour's Tower, with a buttressed crown spire with clock [79]; the reconstruction was carried out in 1624–28, and Galloway was assisted by the masons Bazhen Ogurtsov and William Graf. Soon, however, such Continental links would be outstripped by the even more far-flung relations of global empire, with the ending of the age of the peripatetic professional Scot in Europe, and the dawning of the new age of Scotland as a partner in British imperialism.

78 Tain Tolbooth, Easter Ross, by Alexander Stronach, 1706–8: this three-storey ashlar tower-house maintained the old-fashioned pattern into the 18th century. (The present clock was installed in 1877.)

79 Spassky or St Saviour's Tower, in the wall of the Kremlin, Moscow, reconstructed and heightened by Christopher Galloway, assisted by Bazhen Ogurtsov and William Graf, 1624–28.

One of the Fronts of the Royal Pallace as Design'd
for the Preceeding Plans

Extends. 144

Gul Adam delin

R Cooper Sculp

Chapter 4   The 18th Century: Age of Improvement

Modernity and Antiquity

The first four decades following the parliamentary union with England in 1707 saw a continuation of intermittent civil war and economic stagnation. The Hanoverian succession of 1714 reinforced the Presbyterian ascendancy and provoked a series of invasions and uprisings by the 'Jacobites' – the party of the exiled Stuarts – with the aim of reestablishing an absolutist monarchy and Episcopalian Protestantism (or even Catholicism). Following the final defeat of Jacobitism in 1746, the nation's prospects changed radically in the second half of the century. The old feudal, hierarchical society was revolutionized by market capitalism, with its emphasis on individualistic risk-taking, and the Enlightenment held out the hope that people could exert control over their environment and over the course of history, if the lessons of scientific enquiry were harnessed rationally. Scotland in the 18th century was a largely self-governing society – not in a formal, legislative sense, but because of the Hanoverian Whig ascendancy's dislike of state centralism, which they associated with Britain's Catholic, Continental enemies. And Scotland's key role in providing the administrators, soldiers and commercial entrepreneurs needed by the growing British empire meant that this small country was now entering its time of greatest international influence, which would last until World War I.

In the rural and urban environment, the combined effect of Enlightenment and market forces was a controlled social and economic transformation known as 'Improvement', replacing informal subsistence with commercial structures. It was first adumbrated in England in the early 18th century; but from the 1750s onwards, the cause of Improvement was taken up by Scottish landowners and turned into an impassioned, indigenous

80 Lord Mar: design for a 'Royal Palace', 1720s, as later published in William Adam's *Vitruvius Scoticus*.

crusade. Architecture's main role was to establish spatial order, as part of the Enlightenment aspiration to shape human behaviour through the environment. Along with activities such as mapping and statistics, it formed part of a new campaign of peaceful control, through the reshaping of the old farming landscape and the building of new settlements. Later in the century this utilitarian rationalism provoked a creative counter-reaction in the form of the Romantic movement, emphasizing the irrational qualities of nature.

The Scottish landscape of Improvement was thickly peopled with fervent innovators, committed to its ethos of constant struggle and change. Most were improver–lairds, men like Sir John Sinclair of Ulbster, who implemented a prodigious programme of agricultural improvement in his native Caithness at the end of the century [97], along with national initiatives such as the publication of the Statistical Account volumes. The pioneers also included the principal architects of the day, notably the Adam family, whose activities over two generations reflected the Improvement trend towards ever greater ambition and specialization. Early 18th-century Scottish architecture and construction were dominated by the irrepressible entrepreneurial enterprises of William Adam (1689–1748), industrialist, contractor, quarrymaster, landowner – and building designer. A champion of Whig mercantilism who was equally at home erecting forts for the Hanoverian army and advising aristocrats on the classical reshaping of their castles, Adam was not an architect in today's sense: the first generation of Improvers could not be pedantically pigeonholed. But his talented sons, John (1721–92), Robert (1728–92) and James (1732–94), were more modern in their combination of artistic personality with professional work-practices.

The prodigiously talented Robert Adam, in particular, showed how ambitious Presbyterian Scots could apply Enlightenment lessons in the context of rising British power, to achieve hitherto unheard-of international status. In the 1750s Robert spent several years in the Mediterranean to advance his career with the prestige conferred by direct archaeological investigation of classical remains; he measured the Roman palace at Spalato (Split) in Dalmatia as well as remains in Rome itself, and formed a close friendship with the artists Giovanni Battista Piranesi and Charles-Louis Clérisseau. Returning in 1758 to London rather than Scotland, he became the first architect in Britain to devise a personal, individual style distilled out of both a scholarly knowledge of antiquity and the manipulation of emotions through

Picturesque Romanticism. Practising initially with the assistance of his brother, James (especially between 1763 and 1773), Robert published his Spalato drawings in 1764 (with perspectives by Clérisseau) and his and James's first volume of *Works* in 1773. The emergence of the modern architect–personality could only have happened in London, where, compared to Paris, wealthy private clients, requiring grand but distinctive spaces, were far more dominant. Yet Robert combined this, from 1761, with the salaried official post of Architect of the King's Works – in tandem with his great rival, Sir William Chambers (1723–96).

Chambers, like another influential mid-18th-century neoclassical pioneer, James 'Athenian' Stuart (1713–88), was a second-generation Scot; and generally during the 18th century the phenomenon of talented Scottish architects moving to London became established. However, the growth of Improvement created a counter-pull: in 1750 Robert Adam had complained that Scotland was a 'narrow place' where change was impossible, but by the 1790s there were numerous innovative projects under way, and the 19th century would see the flourishing of a diverse Scottish architectural culture.

In the governing ideas of architecture, the 18th century saw the spread of Enlightenment values. Early in the century, the only debate was over the precise interpretation of classical precedents; no-one realized yet that there was no single unified 'antiquity'. How could the classical ideal be related to the national past? Castellar buildings at first seemed completely unacceptable, and the architect's job was to demolish, hide or remodel them. The 1744 enlargement of Archerfield House, East Lothian, by John Douglas (d. c. 1778) involved planting a classical block in front of the old tower. Or the old house might be regularized, shorn of turrets, and set in a Versailles-like axial landscape. In 1733, William Adam, on a trip to Aberfeldy in Perthshire to build a new military bridge, was commissioned by the Earl of Breadalbane to classicize the nearby Balloch Castle: after he had refaced the main block, added Palladian pavilions, and projected avenues of trees like spokes of a wheel out into the landscape, the house was renamed Taymouth Castle [81] to celebrate its transformation; John Douglas commented approvingly that it 'looks well in its new coat and sash windows'.

Once the Jacobite challenge was banished in 1746, there was a change of heart, and the castellar manner began to enjoy a new popularity for country houses. By the 1760s, in the work of Robert Adam, the 'castle style' was only one of a number of stylistic options, as the old classical hierarchy began to break up under the specialized demands of modern life. With the growth of cultural relativism, one could pick and choose different interpretations of the antique, and combine these with national medievalism; the external style of a building now became essentially a wrapper. With Robert, it was a matter not just of collective relativism but also of artistic individualism, in showpieces such as Kedleston House [88] or Syon House [89, 90]. This eclecticism was part of a wider architectural response to the Enlightenment: it was thought that architecture could directly play on people's minds, not just through its practical function but through the emotional reaction it evoked, especially through the natural 'Sublime' and 'Picturesque'. Although some English Romantic writers began to see nature as opposed to utilitarian Progress, Robert Adam and later Scottish architects exploited the Sublime and Picturesque as an integrated part of Improvement.

All of this might seem to amount to a complete breakdown of classical order. But the last years of the 18th century also witnessed an equally determined attempt to reassert the classical hierarchy of decorum and stateliness by going 'back to basics' in antiquity, in the movement that we today refer to as neoclassicism. The neoclassical ideal of order was expressed in various ways. The first was spatially, by using elemental or repetitive patterns, such as circles or grids. Some of these patterns emphasized control, especially the 'centrical' (in the language of the time) principle of planning settlements or buildings in a radial or centralized fashion, to create a kind of total community and regulate production. The ideal was a new, separate zone of order, such as the Edinburgh New Town [102] or the New Lanark mill village [98]. But the most influential type of town plan remained the time-honoured Roman grid, adjusted to emphasize key axes or buildings. The second main expression of neoclassical order was the rejection of the generalized pre-18th century building formulae – church, palace, etc. – and the invention by architects such as Robert Adam and William Stark (1770–1813) of many new, highly specific building types.

81 Taymouth Castle, Perthshire: detail of a view painted by James Norie in 1733 and modified in 1739 by Jan Griffier II to show recent landscaping alterations. Norie and his sons were key figures in the development of Scottish landscape painting. The view shows the castle and landscape as replanned by William Adam in the 1730s.

The Transformation of Rural Scotland: 'Improving' the Country Seat
It was the Lowland countryside that experienced the first really thoroughgoing programme of Improvement, driven by the landed classes, who were now at the height of their power. The main ingredients of agricultural Improvement concerned new ways of using land. Efficient crop rotation, to increase soil fertility,

required enclosure and amalgamation of the old, communal holdings. The response where architecture and landscape were concerned, from c. 1740 or 1750 onwards, was an eager quest for order. Estates were improved, with rebuilt country houses at their core, new farms planted in the consolidated holdings, and planned villages established to absorb displaced population and provide local services. Once the traditional rural socio-economic order had been overthrown, large numbers of people also moved to towns, and modern urban Scotland began slowly to emerge. The experimental aspects of agricultural Improvement extended to aesthetics: the landscape was a laboratory, whose lessons could be extended to architecture. For example, Lord Kames, an Improvement propagandist in works such as *The Gentleman Farmer* (1774), also influenced Robert Adam through his speculations on the mood-influencing effects of Sublime landscapes.

It was in the designs for the lairds' classical country houses that the contest between different interpretations of antiquity was expressed most forcibly. Internally, the wealth brought by Improvement allowed great sumptuousness in the largest houses, their 'masculine' architectonic order contrasting with the 'feminine' luxury of London and Edinburgh townhouses. Furniture, gilding and landscape painting were kept in tightly controlled arrangements, although the linear state apartment plans were increasingly broken up, and separate large dining and drawing rooms and salons were emphasized. Externally, the late 17th-century Stuart classicism of Bruce and Smith was challenged by other approaches. It had been an offshoot of the hierarchical grandeur of Versailles: a mixture of Baroque drama and Northern European restraint. It had viewed antiquity through the realistic lens of contemporary Continental architecture, and had preferred to incorporate old castellated houses respectfully in remodelling schemes. Under the Hanoverian régime, this cosmopolitan approach could only live on in a shadowy form. Its most talented exponent, John Erskine, 11th Earl of Mar (1675–1732), was one of the chief military leaders in the civil war of 1715–16, in which the Jacobites unsuccessfully attempted to reverse the Hanoverian succession of the previous year. Since the 1690s, Mar had been pursuing an ambitious programme of reconstruction on his estate at Alloa in Clackmannanshire, regularizing the existing castle as the focus of a grand classical landscape, which mingled industrial developments and axial plantations and boulevards. The outflow from his estate loch was used both as a landscape feature and as a power source for his industries in Alloa. In exile after the defeat of his armies, Mar turned to the design of exaggeratedly tall, centrally planned Baroque fantasy palaces [80], intended chiefly for the hoped-for restoration of James Francis Stuart as the British king. A miniature pleasure-garden version of the axial Alloa landscape was constructed at Preston, near Edinburgh, by Mar's brother, Lord Grange, in the years immediately following the 1716 defeat.

For architects with Catholic leanings, the new Hanoverian Protestant age also posed difficulties. For James Smith, this was a time of retrenchment, with relatively modest domestic commissions of the 1710s and 1720s handled jointly with Alexander McGill (d. 1734). After designing a series of fortified garrisons in the Highlands (1718–19), Smith was dismissed, protesting vainly, from his post as architect to the Board of Ordnance in 1719. The Aberdonian James Gibbs (1682–1754), a Catholic, had gone to Rome in 1703 to study for the priesthood, but instead became a pupil of Carlo Fontana, obtaining an experience of contemporary Italian Baroque practice that marks him as unique among British architects. When he returned in 1709 he established himself in London. His work shows a gradual move away from Baroque complexity (in his first church, St Mary-le-Strand, London, 1714–17) towards a more 'august' Roman gravity [99]. Most of his English country houses are monumentally severe on the outside, while sumptuously decorated internally. Equally 'antique' is the style of King's College New Building, Cambridge (1724–49), with thermal window and portico at the centre of its austere main façade.

In England, the early 18th century saw the rise of a new grouping in rivalry to Gibbs, which claimed to harness antiquity directly, bypassing contemporary Continental classicism. This was

82 Colen Campbell: elevation of the initial proposal for Wanstead House, Essex, 1714, from Campbell's *Vitruvius Britannicus*. Campbell's declared aim in this pioneering Palladian composition, with porticoes on both entrance and garden façades, was 'to introduce the Temple Beauties in a Private Building'. This austerely rectangular design was superseded, as built in 1715–20, by a more variegated profile, with a shorter main block and low wings.

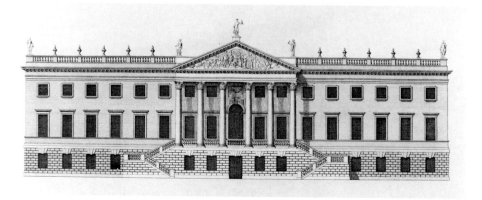

83 House of Dun, Angus, by
Lord Mar with William Adam (and
Alexander McGill), begun in 1743:
the saloon. This room is the focus
of Joseph Enzer's remarkable
Jacobite plasterwork cycle, which
portrays the Augustan peace that
would follow the overthrow of the
Hanoverian regime and restoration
of Stuart rule.

84 Hopetoun House, West
Lothian: the entrance façade, by
William Adam (from 1721)
followed by his sons, led by John
(from 1742). This front was built
across the house designed by Sir
William Bruce (which survives in
part behind).

to be done by looking to the works of the 16th-century Italian architect Palladio, synthesized with the indigenous inspiration of Inigo Jones (architect to James VI & I and Charles I), who had himself been an admirer of Palladio. A key role in this polemical 'Palladian' movement was played by Colen Campbell (1676–1729), a Scot from a landed background who had trained as an advocate before turning to architecture. In 1712 he moved to London, where he published a collection of engravings celebrating the 'British' tradition of classicism, *Vitruvius Britannicus* (1715–25), and designed Wanstead House in Essex [82] (1714–20), the first English country house to feature the grandeur of a porticoed, temple-like main block. Although Campbell sternly attacked the 'affected and licentious' Continental Baroque, ironically these concepts were greatly indebted to the earlier experiments of James Smith in centralized villa planning (see p. 86).

It seems unlikely that any of these architectural tendencies corresponded to specific political Whig or Jacobite positions. Rather, there was much common ground, as seen in the work of William Adam, a staunch Whig upholder of the new régime who was nevertheless careful to hedge his bets until the decisive war of 1745–46, and whose houses drew on the rhetorically expressive designs of Smith and Gibbs alongside English Palladianism. Adam maintained close relations with Lord Mar: a protracted exchange of proposals between Mar, Adam and McGill from 1723 for the ambitious small House of Dun, Angus, built by Adam for a Jacobite kinsman, resulted in 1742–43 in the adoption of a Mar plan for a compact pavilion with a portico in the form of a triumphal arch. Adam supervised the construction of this house, with its allegorical Jacobite plasterwork [83], at the same time as he was busy building military fortifications and roads across the Highlands for the Hanoverian régime.

The catholicity of William Adam's classical country-house architecture is exemplified in his two major works of the 1720s and 1730s: Hopetoun in West Lothian and Duff in Banffshire. In 1721, the Earl of Hopetoun called in Adam to help him recast Bruce's complicated design with a more stately, Versailles-like main front [84], to provide a fitting setting for his celebrated picture collection. Behind the array of giant pilasters are two matching apartments of luxurious double-height rooms, their doors aligned in strict enfilade. The completion and fitting out of this great palace was only finally accomplished by William's sons after his death. But Adam also hankered after the Mar style of highly vertical house [80], and in 1735–40 he was able to realize that ideal in the building of Duff House [87] for Lord Braco. The pilasters of Hopetoun reappear (he bragged that 'they gave the front a grand appearance'), but the state apartments are condensed into a cruciform plan, and the façades terminate in tall, narrow angle turrets. Similarly theatrical in character is Chatelherault, a hunting lodge William built in 1731–42 as a terminal feature for the great south vista of Hamilton Palace: it comprised a screen wall linking two pairs of tall, pedimented pavilions [85].

At the other extreme of scale, William Adam also developed the Smith tradition of the compact, refined villa at Mavisbank, Midlothian (1723–26) [86], where he worked in collaboration with the owner, the influential improving laird and arbiter of taste, Sir John Clerk of Penicuik (1675–1755). With its tiny curved wings, Mavisbank is a microcosm of the pan-British Palladian villa pattern: the early 18th century was still a time of close links with, even dependency on, the architecture of 'South Britain', and after William's death, his sons continued to design houses on the same general plan. The most refined of these was Paxton House in Berwickshire (1759–63), designed probably by John and James on the basis of drawings by the English Palladian architect Isaac Ware (d. 1766), and executed by John's friend, the mason James Nisbet (d. 1781). Although modest in scale, Paxton has a Doric-porticoed main façade of unusual grandeur, commanding a panorama of the Scottish-English border.

85 Chatelherault, Lanarkshire, by William Adam, 1731–42. This ducal hunting lodge, with kennels behind, contains rich plasterwork of 1740–42 by Thomas Clayton.

The East View of Mavisbank House Toward the Court in the County of Mid Lothian one of the Seats of Sʳ John Clerk of Pennycook Baron of his Majesty's Exchequer

86 William Adam and Sir John Clerk of Penicuik:
front elevation of Mavisbank House, Midlothian,
1723–26, from *Vitruvius Scoticus*. The two-storey-and-
basement pavilion in the centre contains a spirally
planned family apartment with a great apartment
above; flanking it are quadrant wings in the
English Palladian manner.

87 Duff House, Banff, by William Adam, 1735–40.

88 Kedleston House, Derbyshire, remodelled by Robert Adam from 1761: the triumphal arch centrepiece of the south or garden façade, 1768. Above it rises the Pantheon dome of the saloon. Adam was engaged by Sir Nathaniel Curzon to remodel a scheme by James Paine (and, previously, Matthew Brettingham).

on pp. 108–9

89 Syon House, near London, reconstructed by Robert Adam from 1762: the anteroom. At Syon the 'Adam' manner was established at the outset of Robert's career, and in its most opulent and variegated form. The sumptuous anteroom is unusually three-dimensional, with its freestanding Ionic columns supporting chunks of entablature – a motif from triumphal arches (cf. ill. 88) and such ancient Roman buildings as the Forum of Nerva – here holding gilded copies of antique statues, and gilt plaster panels based on the antique 'Trophy of Marius' in Rome. The rich ceiling and even richer floor echo each other in overall composition – a device often found in Adam interiors. This highly colourful room is entered from an austerely monochrome columned entrance hall (visible through the doorway), with further copies of antique statues.

90 Syon House: the long gallery. Adam's most difficult challenge was the Jacobean long gallery, and his response was to flatten the architectural elements and impose repetitive patterns of pilasters and geometrical panels; the decoration was derived from 1st- and 2nd-century AD Roman patterns.

From the mid-18th century, the fragmentation of antique authority and the beginning of eclecticism allowed landowners and architects to seek a greater individuality. Within the classical world, Robert Adam's work following his return to London in 1758 – from 1763 with his brother James – established a new, emotionalistic approach to the use of monumental and decorative Roman elements in specific contexts: the first phase of neoclassicism. While the work of his chief rival, Chambers, was characterized by francophile cosmopolitanism (seen in Scotland chiefly in his porticoed villa of 1763–68, Duddingston House, near Edinburgh), Robert Adam remained within the mainstream British tradition of direct engagement with Italian antiquity. However, he rejected Palladianism and the reverence for Inigo Jones as 'ponderous . . . sterile and disgustful', and against it set the dramatic contrasts of what he called 'movement', a concept of building profile influenced by the ideas of the Picturesque and Sublime, which was his governing principle of design. Robert and James summed it up in 1773, in Volume I of their Works, as follows: 'Movement is meant to express, the rise and fall, the advance and recess, with other diversity of form, in the different parts of a building, so as to add greatly to the picturesque of a composition . . . the same effect in architecture, that hill and dale, foreground and distance, swelling and sinking have in landscape.' 'Movement' was seen at its closest to the Baroque in Robert's remodelling from 1761 of Kedleston House in Derbyshire, which features a centrepiece on the garden façade based on the Arch of Constantine in Rome [88]. Inside, there is a grand columned hall, and a saloon beneath a coffered Pantheon dome. The Adams boasted in their Works that 'we really do not recollect any example of so much movement and contrast, as in the south front of Kedleston house'.

Many of Robert Adam's English projects were for the reshaping internally of existing houses – a brief familiar to any Scottish classical architect. But he rejuvenated this task with an internal version of 'movement', contrasting monumental elements with a new low-relief decorative plasterwork style based on the 'grotesque' ornament of ancient Roman domestic architecture as mediated by Raphael and other 16th-century painters. 'Movement' was also accentuated by the diversity of room plans, their varied shapes derived especially from Roman baths and palaces. Adam's most theatrical differentiation of rooms by style and shape in this 'antique' manner is at Syon House near London, remodelled for the Duke of Northumberland from 1762: here the treatment

ranges from the extreme architectonic opulence of the anteroom
[89], ringed with statue-crowned freestanding columns (some
imported Roman originals), to the low-relief detail of the long
gallery, 'in a style to afford great variety and amusement' [90].

By the 1770s, the spread of Improvement in Scotland allowed
Adam to build on a grand scale back home. From the mid-1770s,
he increasingly indulged his leanings towards pictorial eclecticism,
including a more extravagantly monumental classicism, and (as we
shall see) a castellated style for country houses. His later classical
projects included the great palace of Gosford House in East
Lothian [91], overlooking the Forth, built in 1790–1803 to house

91 Gosford House, East Lothian, by Robert Adam, 1790–1803. The original Greek-cross-plan pavilion wings were replaced by the present larger structures as part of a florid enlargement by William Young in 1891. The central block, with its dome and three monumental interiors behind the three vast columned windows, was left largely intact, though rearranged about a longitudinal circulation route.

the Earl of Wemyss in the style of the Emperor Diocletian at Spalato. The domed main block contains three great rooms at the front, each with a vast arched window, intended to illuminate the Earl's famous picture collection.

The Adam style of eclectic house planning and decoration was the first Scottish architectural movement to exert a widespread international influence – notably through the works of Charles Cameron (1745–1812), a designer of Scottish descent, for Catherine the Great of Russia, including lavish apartments for the Empress in the main palace and several smaller buildings in the park of Tsarskoye Selo (1779–87). However, by the time of Robert's death in 1792, his empiricism had been overtaken internationally by the more militant second phase of neoclassicism, relying especially on Greek, rather than Roman, inspiration, and emphasizing elemental, geometrical building forms. In Scotland, the rationalist aspects of this phase of neoclassicism were expressed mainly in the planning of institutional buildings. Stylistically, extreme geometrical neoclassicism is largely confined to the work of the short-lived James Playfair (1755–94) in the 1790s, notably Cairness House, Aberdeenshire (1788–93) [92], built for the heir to a Jamaica sugar fortune. Cairness, in its combination of rigorous geometry and exotic eclecticism, prefigured key trends of early 19th-century Scottish country house architecture. Its main block, starkly built in granite, with its underplayed centre and flanking cubic towers, contains (among other interiors) an 'Egyptian' billiard room with hieroglyphic detail and battered door and fireplace surrounds. To the rear is a semi-circular court of offices of even more elemental design. Playfair's later and even more exaggeratedly neoclassical Lynedoch Mausoleum at Methven, Perthshire (1793), resembles a Greek temple composed out of horizontal strips.

Alongside the fragmentation of the antique ideal, the old tension between classical and castellated began to re-emerge in the late 18th century – only in a different form, shaped by the Enlightenment preoccupation with the use of architecture to shape the emotions. This new movement had already begun to emerge outside and around the classical house, in the development of a contrasting natural setting and the movement for informal, wild landscaping. Bruce had incorporated a castle ruin with Jacobite associations into an axial vista at Kinross in the 1680s; but it was not until the 1740s that the decisive step was taken of building a completely new castle. This was first done not by a Jacobite but by one of the chief Whig lairds, the 3rd Duke of Argyll – and in the mid-1740s, at the climax of the Hanoverian–Stuart dynastic struggle. In those years, the Duke began a vast programme of estate improvement at his seat of Inveraray [93]. As part of this, to symbolize his status as tenant-in-chief to the Crown and to assert the Scottish credentials of Hanoverian and Presbyterian power, he decided to build a grand

92 Cairness House, Aberdeenshire, by James Playfair, 1788–93. The sparkling granite house is clasped by a curved court of offices (rusticated to show its 'service' character), which terminates on either side in a lower façade with a thermal window.

new house for himself, set in axial landscaping but in a castellated style. After rejecting a design like a bastion-ringed fortlet from the military engineer Dugal Campbell (d. 1757), he engaged the English architect Roger Morris (1695–1749) to produce a simpler design, symmetrical with corner turrets and central lantern tower. Inevitably, William Adam was deeply involved in this seminal project, advising Morris on the design, and actually building the house in 1746–49 after the Jacobite defeat.

But it was only later in the century, at the hands of Robert Adam, that the castle style could truly begin to flourish. He integrated it with the new Sublime concepts of landscaping, and with his own picturesque design principle of 'movement', and introduced specifically Scottish castle features. The Enlightenment ideal of historical progress was complemented by an antiquarian fascination with the pre-Hanoverian Scottish past, along with a romantic aestheticization of the Highland landscape and its people, as epitomized by the Ossian poems of James MacPherson (a client of Adam). Robert Adam gave architectural form to these ideas from c. 1770 in a series of new or remodelled castles, asymmetrical in profile although composed of symmetrical elements, and often set in Sublime locations. However, the sources of this castle style were as much classical as national, as it was inspired partly by the castles that appear in the Italian landscape paintings of the 17th-century artists Poussin and Claude. Inside, the houses follow Adam's standard classical formula, with its contrasting room shapes. The greatest triumph of his romantic castle style was Culzean, a compact group built from 1777 on an Ayrshire clifftop [94]. Here, in 1785, Adam added a new façade looking out to sea, with a grand circular saloon at its centre; externally, this is expressed as a round bastion on a vaulted base, towering over the crags.

New patterns of agriculture and settlement
Throughout the Lowlands, the 18th-century replanning of the farming landscape consigned to oblivion the old, jumbled townships of turf byre-houses. In its place, there developed an orderly, consolidated pattern of large rectangular fields, studded with neat stone courtyard steadings and farmhouses like small classical villas – a pattern of extraordinary consistency, fuelled by the numerous Improvement agricultural societies. To house the displaced population and provide markets and specialist trades for improved agriculture, over a hundred new towns were founded in the 18th century across Scotland, and almost the same number

93 Inveraray, Argyll: panoramic view of the landscape as 'improved' by the 3rd Duke of Argyll, with the castle on the right, and the new town on the promontory to the left. The castle, by Roger Morris, was built in 1746–49. The town was designed by John Adam and others, and begun in the 1750s; Robert Mylne's church, of temple form, stands in the middle of the peninsula.

94 Culzean Castle, Ayrshire, by Robert Adam, begun in 1777: aerial view showing the dramatic clifftop situation of the new frontage of 1785, with its circular bastion looking out to sea, and the service courtyard, integrated into the overall design, on the left.

again in 1800–1840. The ultimate source of the ethos of rectilinear planted settlements was colonialism and military campaigning, whether in ancient Rome or modern Europe. Now, reinvigorated by the Enlightenment, it was put to the service of Hanoverian mercantilism. Unlike English landowners' model villages, every new Scottish settlement was from the start seen as an embryonic town. The pioneers, appropriately, were in East Lothian: Yester (now Gifford), built from 1708 by the 2nd Marquess of Tweeddale, and the nearby village of Ormiston, started by John Cockburn c. 1740 as a focus of linen manufacture. By 1750, the movement had spread to the north-east, with the foundation of New Keith by the Earl of Findlater, planned with four parallel streets and a wide central space.

In the Highlands, the challenge was far greater, and stimulated more extreme solutions. At first, in the troubled early 18th century, Improvement and military pacification were closely bound together, in the road-building activities of General George Wade from 1724, and the map-surveying work of General William Roy from 1747. The culmination of this programme was the building of a complete fortified garrison town, Fort George, near Inverness, in 1748–69 [96], designed by the English engineer Colonel William Skinner (1700–1780) and built, inevitably, by William Adam and his sons. This sublimely symmetrical layout, ringed by gigantic bastions, was a last resounding gesture in the Renaissance tradition of grand formal fortification: from then on, military building ceased to be 'architecture'.

Only after the Jacobite defeat could the plantation of new civilian settlements in the Highlands begin. The 3rd Duke of Argyll's works around Inveraray led the way, in their integration of country-house building with agricultural remodelling. From c. 1750, the Duke began the clearance of Glen Aray and Glen Shira for improved cattle farming, and in 1787 Robert Mylne (1733–1811), then working on the classical interiors at Inveraray Castle, designed a novel steading at Maam [95], in the form of a castellated circle; only half was eventually built. The Duke's improvement programme required both the displacement of a large rural population and the relocation of the existing burgh of Inveraray. The appropriate 'centrical' response was to build a new classical town [93]: the cruciform layout and main frontage were designed in the 1750s by John Adam, and later buildings were infilled by Mylne, including a centrally placed church (1795–1802).

As the town-planting movement spread across the Highlands, the lairds generally laid out the streets and lots, but left

95 Robert Mylne: Maam Steading, Argyll. An engraving by John Smith from the *General View of Agriculture of the County of Argyll* shows the internal and external elevations and the plan proposed for this circular farm, one of the showpieces of the 3rd Duke's vast improvement drive. By the date of the engraving only half had been built, in 1787–90; the project was never completed.

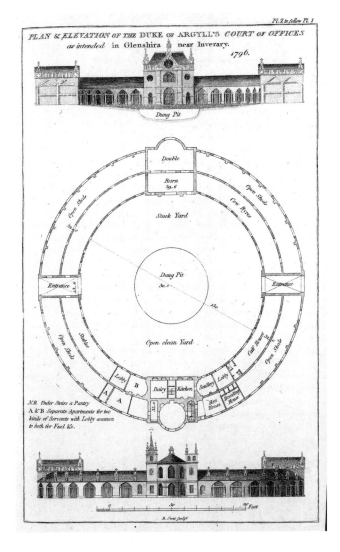

development to the purchasers. Sir James Macdonald of Sleat wrote in 1783 of his new village of Portree, Skye, that he had 'had the whole marked with a plough that the city may be founded in the true classical way'. To provide employment for surplus population, in 1786 the Highland Society of London set up a new British Fisheries Society, to build new fishing villages: the most important was Ullapool, Ross, where a grid layout was planned by David Aitken in 1787. Some later projects met with mixed success: at Kyleakin on Skye, begun in 1799, of an incongruously grandiose plan of 1811 by the architect James Gillespie Graham

96 Fort George, Inverness-shire, by Colonel William Skinner, 1748–69. Built at a cost of nearly £100,000, the symmetrical fort was an extreme and introverted variant of axial new-town planning, containing severely classical barrack and service blocks arranged in rows and courtyards.

97 Thurso, Caithness: plan for the new town, by Sir John Sinclair of Ulbster, 1798. Four markets and a 'town house' are shown west of the square; industry was grouped by the river. The street layout was implemented, but most of the public buildings remained unbuilt.

98 New Lanark, Lanarkshire, developed from 1783 by David Dale: aerial view of the surviving buildings. This self-contained utopian settlement originally comprised four multi-storey mills, designed in the form of simplified palace-blocks, and streets of tenements to house 2,000 workers; the focus of the village was a school for 510 pupils.

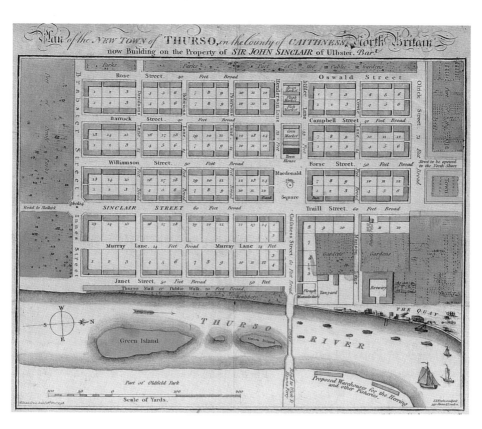

(1776–1855) for rows of houses grouped in pedimented terraces and churches with spires, almost nothing was built. In Caithness, the indefatigable Improver Sir John Sinclair decided in 1798 to build a new town at Thurso [97] with British Fisheries Society subsidy, and commissioned 'the most regular plan that could be contrived', including a grid of residential streets, public buildings and markets.

In general, industry in the 18th century was still a rural matter, and a number of spacious textile mill villages were built from the 1780s, using the cotton-spinning technology developed by the English inventor Richard Arkwright. However, the most important mill village of this series, New Lanark in Lanarkshire [98], had a very different character, being packed densely in the steep glen of the Falls of Clyde. This highly self-contained, even utopian settlement was developed from 1783 by the industrialist David Dale.

Urban Improvement
In existing towns, unlike the countryside, *tabula rasa* solutions were impracticable. The state in Hanoverian Britain, unlike absolutist France, had no power to project vast axes and vistas to create a 'city as monument'. In the insecure conditions of the early 18th century, one could do little more than make do and mend. Public buildings moved away from the tolbooth tradition towards a thoroughgoing classical regularity, shaped by publications such as Gibbs's *Book of Architecture* (1728). Gibbs's church of St Martin-in-the-Fields, London (1722–26) [99], was influential in the way it integrated a steeple, with its traditional burgh overtones, with the antique grandeur of a porticoed temple hall. It shaped not only the design of classical churches, such as St Andrew's, Glasgow, of 1737–59, by Allan Dreghorn (1706–65), but also the civic buildings of the post-tolbooth era, such as William Adam's elegant Dundee Town House (1731–34) [100]. Edinburgh's chief mid-century public building, the new Exchange (1753–61) by John Adam, was promoted by the town council; it ingeniously shoehorned an arcaded and porticoed courtyard group into the hilltop town centre.

In the second half of the century, it at last became possible for urban Improvement to take root. In contrast to the countryside, the main concern of Enlightenment urbanism was not the pursuit of pure centrical order, but segregation of the uses and inhabitants of the town. Work was to be separated from housing, the poor from the rich, and key monuments set apart from the general

99 St Martin-in-the-Fields Church, London, by James Gibbs, 1722–26: a pioneer of the temple-and-steeple formula for religious and public buildings.

100 The Town House, Dundee, Fife, by William Adam, 1731–34. The tower over a pediment shows the influence of St Martin-in-the-Fields; also from Gibbs came the design of the window openings, with alternating rustication. The Town House replaced an old tolbooth; in 1932 it was demolished in its turn to allow the building of the Beaux-Arts classical City Square.

urban fabric. But there was also a growing appreciation of the city as an aesthetic totality. In 1789 Robert Barker, an Edinburgh artist, made the world's first panorama, a giant wrap-round painting of the city seen from Calton Hill [101]. That aesthetic overview was matched by an ethos of public or collective control of development, through alliances of town councils and urban landowning institutions (notably, in Edinburgh, George Heriot's Trust), to lay out new, axial street patterns and set down guidelines for developers.

Much the most important Scottish urban development of the century was the Edinburgh New Town – a new, high-class residential suburb to the north of the Old Town, linked to it by a bridge. Although the general concept had first been suggested by James VII & II, its context now was a civic Hanoverian patriotism: a pamphlet of 1752, *Proposals for Carrying on Certain Public Works in the City of Edinburgh*, emphasized the need to prevent an exodus of the wealthy from the dense Old Town to London. In a competition of 1766–67, the proposal of the young James Craig (1744–95) was accepted, initially for a highly centralized diagonal layout based on the British flag, but later revised into an axial grid [102], with greater emphasis given to key elements. The relationship to the Old Town was critical [101]: the flank facing it became the new suburb's most important street (Princes Street). Behind its classical façades, this first section of the New Town was made up of a mixture of self-contained row houses, on the London model, and apartment flats in slightly less prestigious locations; the only detached villa of note was Chambers's chaste, pedimented block for Sir Laurence Dundas (1771–74), located at the eastern end of

101 Edinburgh, seen from Calton Hill, was the subject of the first 360-degree panorama ever painted, by Robert Barker, in 1789. The full-scale version, exhibited in both Edinburgh and London, was 8 metres (25 feet) in diameter. This detail comes from a smaller-scale copy made in 1792. We are looking west. In the left distance is the Old Town, with the crown spire of St Giles's and the Castle standing out on the ridge. The North Bridge links the Old Town to the new extensions to the north. There we see irregular developments in the foreground (far right in the plan, ill. 102), but beyond them extends the regular grid of Craig's New Town, where the first streets are under construction. Princes Street runs off into the distance beside the loch that separates New Town from Old. Suburban villas dot the countryside north of the city.

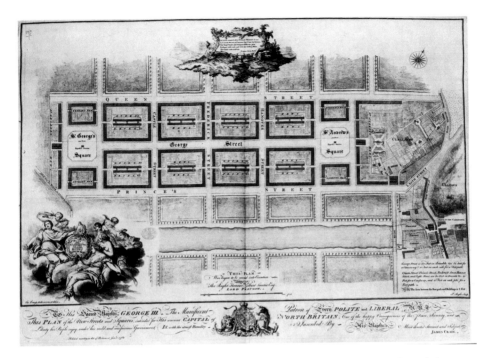

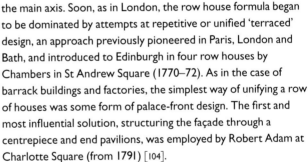

102 Edinburgh New Town:
the adopted plan by James Craig,
July 1767.

the main axis. Soon, as in London, the row house formula began to be dominated by attempts at repetitive or unified 'terraced' design, an approach previously pioneered in Paris, London and Bath, and introduced to Edinburgh in four row houses by Chambers in St Andrew Square (1770–72). As in the case of barrack buildings and factories, the simplest way of unifying a row of houses was some form of palace-front design. The first and most influential solution, structuring the façade through a centrepiece and end pavilions, was employed by Robert Adam at Charlotte Square (from 1791) [104].

The parallel Georgian development of London was constantly in the mind of the Edinburgh designers, not least because Robert Adam was so deeply involved there. In the early 1770s, he had carried out numerous sumptuous commissions for the remodelling of aristocrats' London townhouses, such as 20 St James's Square (1771–74), Derby House (1773–74), Home House (1773–76), and, most lavish of all, the glass drawing room of Northumberland House (1770). But the Whig mercantile spirit also fuelled numerous speculative developments involving the brothers, of which by far the boldest was the gigantic Adelphi redevelopment of 1768–71 [103] – a complex of dwellings on a vaulted commercial base, on the north side of the Thames.

103 The Adelphi development, London, by Robert and James Adam, 1768–71. The Adams' *Works in Architecture* shows the frontage to the Thames, with St Paul's Cathedral in the distance. In this multi-level complex, houses, flats and professional chambers rose above a vaulted commercial base, which included 'cottage' dwellings in the substructures; the river façade, with its end terraces at right angles, was composed as if it were a palace front flanked by pavilions. 'Adelphi Terrace' was indeed raised on a terrace; but from here the term was taken to describe all rows of linked houses.

104 The north side of Charlotte Square, Edinburgh, by Robert Adam, begun in 1791: one of the earliest examples in Scotland of the unified 'palace' design of a terrace of houses.

This multi-level concept then, in turn, stimulated Edinburgh developments, notably the South Bridge to the south of the Old Town: Adam's 1785 vision of a 'viaduct-street' flanked by colonnaded shops and housing to a unified design was built in simplified form in 1786–88 by Robert Kay (1740–1818).

In the two other main Scottish urban centres, Glasgow and Aberdeen, the unified development controls of Edinburgh were lacking, and thus there could be no total, centrical development like the New Town. In Glasgow, the response was a Roman-style, open-ended grid formula, suitable for any pace and scale of development. This was first seen on a 1782 plan by the land surveyor James Barry. It had become standard by the time the first suburbs south of the River Clyde, Trades Town (1791) and Hutcheson Town (1794), were begun, and James Craig had drawn up a plan for a large western residential extension on the Blythswood estate. In Aberdeen, where the town centre was fragmented by numerous sharp hills, the chief unifying response was the projection of a new linking boulevard to the south-west, Union Street (built from 1801) [147] – a somewhat less dramatic version of Edinburgh's South Bridge. Aberdeen had not yet developed into a 'Granite City': the first granite building of dressed ashlar, James Brown's Aberdeen Banking Company, Castle Street, was only built in 1801–2.

Enlightenment urban development was a matter not just of street layouts and rows of houses, but of new institutional building types. Traditional types such as the palace or the church were adapted with the chief monumental motifs of antiquity, such as the triumphal arch or the Pantheon dome. The result was a complex pattern of overlaps, between types as disparate as parliament buildings, libraries and prisons. The pioneering architectural work was largely by Robert and James Adam, who easily adopted the variegated principle of 'movement', as at Kedleston [88], to an urban institutional context. Following a succession of influential but abortive proposals by James in the 1760s for a palace-like classical reconstruction of the Westminster parliament complex [105], Robert, as government architect, was awarded the commission for the first large Scottish state building commenced in the 18th century: General Register House, a centre of government records at the east end of the Edinburgh New Town [106]. Started by Adam in 1774 and completed in 1822–34 by his successor, Robert Reid, it comprises a domed Pantheon-style

105 James Adam: unexecuted proposal for the reconstruction of the parliament and law courts complex in Westminster, London, c. 1763 (elevation drawing possibly reworked by Charles-Louis Clérisseau). The project envisaged a vast domed rotunda flanked by parliamentary chambers and courtyards, with porticoes on all four sides. This formula was widely influential, and helped shape, for example, the competition-winning design of 1793 for the United States Capitol in Washington, D.C., by the Scottish-educated architect and painter William Thornton.

106 General Register House, Edinburgh, begun in 1774 by Robert Adam, and completed in 1822–34 (with blocks at the rear) by Robert Reid.

107 University College, Edinburgh, by Robert Adam, begun in 1789: detail of the triumphal arch entrance portico, with six giant monoliths of Craigleith stone. Adam wrote in 1789 of 'this great and important Work, which I had so much at heart', as 'a monument of my talents, such as they are'.

reading room rotunda enclosed in a quadrangle of offices, with a restrained, porticoed façade. A courtyard plan was adopted by Adam for the new Edinburgh University College, commenced in 1789 at one end of the new South Bridge. The main façade has a triumphal arch entrance, with tall monolithic columns [107].

In buildings for control and for reform of the poor, the main task was seen as that of surveillance and guidance, combining utilitarian efficiency with evangelical zeal. The Panopticon, a radial plan allowing surveillance from one central point, published by the English reformer Jeremy Bentham in 1791, was reflected in Robert Adam's 1791 design for a new Edinburgh Bridewell prison, incorporating the 'principle of invisible inspection' in a semi-circular, radially planned arrangement of cells; externally the prison was not classical but in Adam's castle style. Later, from the 1800s, the neoclassical architect William Stark would develop these ideas in astylar classical form, notably in his Glasgow lunatic asylum designed in 1804–6 (built 1807–20, now demolished) [108], with its Greek cross plan, central drum and dome, and segregated exercise yards all around, so that 'each class may be formed into a society inaccessible to all others'; Stark's subsequent Dundee asylum (1812–20) was lower and more domestic in character.

Conclusion
In the matching of building types and forms to the demands of a modernizing age, the 18th century saw the emergence of a new spirit of experimentation in Scottish architecture. In the 19th century, as the pace of modernization quickened and its scope broadened further, that ethos of restless innovation and creativity would become all-pervasive.

108 Glasgow Asylum, by William Stark, designed 1804–6, built 1807–20. One of a succession of large institutional projects influenced by the 'Panopticon' principle of centralized planning for surveillance and classification. This photograph shows it c. 1900, by which time it had been extended by the wing at the right.

109 Gardner Warehouse, Glasgow, by John Baird I (with the iron-founder R. McConnel), 1855–56. The patented prefabricated iron structural system permits a range of subtleties of detailing.

Chapter 5 The 19th Century: High Summer of Scottish Architecture

Where Chapter 4 traced the growth of Improvement, this chapter tells of its comprehensive realization. The years after 1815 saw the beginning of half a century's untrammelled capitalist expansion. The final British victory in the Napoleonic wars was followed, in Scotland, by a period of unprecedented growth on all fronts. At home, the population rose by 15 per cent during the 1820s and then doubled again by the end of the century. Urbanization accelerated, especially in the Clyde valley, where it was fuelled by a complex of interlocking industries – coal, iron, textiles and ultimately shipbuilding – and by new rail and deep-sea transport links. Domestic growth was also closely interrelated with the triumphal march of British imperialism: hundreds of thousands of Scots fanned out across the empire, whether as ordinary workers and farmers (especially in Canada and New Zealand) or as part of the commercial, administrative, and spiritual élites – as exemplified by the tireless missionary explorations of David Livingstone. The social conflicts unleashed by this growth, and by the political franchise reforms of 1832 and 1868, swept away the remnants of feudal society: from the 1830s the Liberals enjoyed effective ascendancy for the remainder of the century, while the Church of Scotland, the 'national Kirk', was split in two by the 'Disruption' of 1843, when an independent-minded, middle-class minority formed the new Free Church of Scotland. There were health crises, too, in town and country alike: during the 1830s, '40s and '50s, for instance, the teeming cities were struck by epidemics of cholera, typhus and typhoid, and the West Highlands by a potato famine. In response, the second half of the century saw an increasing tendency towards collective, public action: for example, in the 1872 Education Act, which set up a world-class system of free, compulsory schooling, or in the 1885 reestablishment of the post of Scottish Secretary to represent Scotland directly within central government – the beginning of the process of political 'home rule' that continues today.

But all in all, despite the many problems, from the perspective of the time the picture was one of ebullient confidence. Scotland enjoyed almost complete internal autonomy, and there was also a host of regional and civic–urban cultural identities, as well as a flamboyant individualism – all in all, a diversity never equalled before or since. In the mushrooming cities, and above all in Glasgow, the nation's Victorian powerhouse, the proliferation of secular organizations, private and public, was paralleled by an explosion in religious proselytizing. In the countryside, the agrarian revolution was brought to mechanized maturity.

For the built environment, this time of ferment was uniquely stimulating: this proved to be the 'golden century' of Scottish architecture – the time of its greatest prosperity and creativity. Arguably, the most striking development of this period was not the innovations of high stylistic fashion but the vast expansion in substantial 'everyday building', applying to the built environment as a whole the scientific lessons of the Enlightenment. Previously, there had been a polarization between the masonry of élite buildings and the flimsy turf or wooden materials of utility structures. Now polished ashlar facing spread even to the average tenements and commercial buildings of the Victorian city. And it became possible to embed within this environment many new and experimental building types, often openly using metal construction – notably in the huge spans of bridges or railway termini (such as the arched Glasgow Queen Street terminus of 1878–80 by the engineer James Carsewell), or in the repetitive spaces of commercial buildings, translated notably into a round-arched, loosely Renaissance form in the exposed iron frame of John Baird I's Gardner Warehouse, Jamaica Street, Glasgow (1855–56; designed with the ironfounder and patentee R. McConnel) [109].

This 'golden century' was stamped from beginning to end by the daring of experimental engineering construction: no obstacle to the march of improvement and British power now seemed insuperable. One of its earliest and noblest monuments, the Bell Rock Lighthouse, stands on a storm-blasted reef off the Angus coast. Designed by Robert Stevenson (1772–1850), founder of an international dynasty of lighthouse engineers, this great tower with concave tapering sides, assembled in appalling weather conditions in 1807–11 out of 2,835 precisely designed stone

110 Skerryvore Lighthouse, near Tiree, by Alan Stevenson (engineer to the Northern Lighthouse Board), 1838–44. The £90,000 tower, whose outer face is gently battered in the form of a hyperbolic curve, is built of granite ashlar on a gneiss base.

segments, presents an integrated image of neoclassical elegance. It was followed by a succession of even more audacious projects by Robert Stevenson and his son Alan (1807–65), culminating in the granite tower 45 metres (148 feet) high built by the latter in 1838–44 at Skerryvore, off the island of Tiree [110].

More generally, however, 19th-century architecture avoided a close integration of engineering and architectural elements in tackling its new tasks. Higher architectural value was seen rather as something added to a building carcase through ornament and style. But access to that added value was widened to an unprecedented degree. No longer was a Grand Tour necessary for the aspiring architect: the required information was all directly accessible through the proliferation of published source-books. As the brightest of Scotland's 19th-century architectural stars, Alexander Thomson (1817–75), argued in 1859, 'If an architect wants an idea, he does not require to fly away into the region of imagination to fetch it – it is ready to hand on the adjoining shelf, and needs only to be fetched down.' The meanings of buildings, including the elevated, almost sacred status of the new, grand secular institutions, were expressed through the connotations of different styles. This eclecticism formed part of a wider breakdown of the European consensus of taste that had prevailed since the late 17th century, shifting from specific and unified styles, such as Gothic or Grecian, to more hybrid or individualized formulas. The most obvious practical effect was the juxtaposition of many different styles in the everyday street, with buildings differentiated by mass-produced ornament. But in opposition to that chaotic diversity, architects such as Thomson attempted a novel kind of emotional and subjective intensity, fighting commercial mass ornament through the development of personal ethical philosophies and styles.

National Architectures

Of all the meanings conveyed by the styles of the 19th century, the most direct and elevated was that of national identity. Scotland's aspiration to a special status within Britain and the empire was a constant concern of the age, and it was largely through the novels of Sir Walter Scott in the 1810s and 1820s that Scottish identity became inextricably associated with the romantic Highland past. But the architectural styles used to express that aspiration changed constantly and radically, and the dominant one during most of Scott's own career was something remote from tartan pageantry: Greek classicism. Across Europe, the archaeological

III Panorama of Edinburgh from the Castle, looking north-east, in 1935. In the foreground, from left to right, are the Royal Institution (1822–35; now the Royal Scottish Academy) and National Gallery of Scotland (1850–58), both by W. H. Playfair. In the background, from left to right, are the Sir Walter Scott Monument (G. Meikle Kemp, 1840–46); the North British Hotel (William Hamilton Beattie, 1892–96); Calton Hill and the columns of the National Monument (W. H. Playfair with C. R. Cockerell, 1821–29); the Bank of Scotland (David Bryce, 1864–70); and the Free Church College (W. H. Playfair, 1846–50).

112 Royal High School, Edinburgh, by Thomas Hamilton, 1825–29. This view shows it in the 1880s with the Calton Hill monuments and prison in the background.

rediscovery of Greece had gone hand in hand with the emergence of modern nationalism; for post-1815 Britain, the self-styled liberator of Europe, the Athens of Themistocles seemed a special inspiration. William Stark, alongside more floridly monumental classical work such as his domed, Corinthian-columned nave-and-aisles hall for the Signet (Upper) Library, Edinburgh, from 1812 [140], had already played a key role in propagating the Grecian fashion in Scottish architecture, notably in a new municipal headquarters of 1809–14 for burgeoning Glasgow, whose heavy hexastyle portico and pilastered pavilions pioneered the giant Greek Doric order in Scotland. But it was on Edinburgh's Calton Hill, dominated by Adam's frowning Bridewell prison, that the buildings most expressive of Scotland's dual national identity sprang up [III, 112, 173]. The first was a 'National Monument' to the dead soldiers of the Napoleonic wars, proposed in 1816. For this triumphal task, it was decided in 1821 that only an exact copy of the Parthenon would suffice, superintended by the English neoclassicist C. R. Cockerell (1788–1863) and an up-and-coming

Edinburgh Grecian, William Henry Playfair (1789–1857). In 1829, after only twelve columns had been built, the project ran out of money and was abandoned, but Calton Hill continued to evolve from a penal colony and military redoubt into a Scottish intellectual acropolis, framed by a Propylaea-like complex of stepped Doric porticoes and colonnades designed for the prestigious Royal High School of 1825–29 by another Edinburgh neoclassicist, Thomas Hamilton (1784–1858) [112].

By the 1830s, neo-Greek had become a general style of national authority and educational enlightenment. But by then there was a rising demand for a more authentic national architecture, based on pre-classical medievalism. In 1822, a visit by George IV was dominated by tartan-clad events orchestrated by Scott, and soon a national monument could only be built in the Gothic style. The monument erected to Scott's memory in Edinburgh in 1840–46 was a Gothic 'temple', situated right beside the classical New Town [111]. The tall spire-like canopy, enshrining a statue of Scott by John Steell, was designed by George Meikle Kemp (1795–1844), a pioneer of the accurate archaeological recording of medieval monuments. From that point, as we shall see shortly, the ecclesiastical associations of Gothic became dominant, whereas for country houses and national secular buildings there was a shift to a more specifically Scottish pre-classical style: the 'Scotch Baronial'. The most spectacular example of a Baronial Valhalla is the National Wallace Monument

(1861–69) near Stirling [113], a rock-faced landmark tower with a crown spire, designed by the Glasgow architect J. T. Rochead (1814–78).

By the closing decades of the century, the great historical styles were no longer seen as clear indicators of identity, and 'national architecture' became more diffuse in style. A new national pantheon, the Scottish National Portrait Gallery of 1884–89 [114], was designed by R. Rowand Anderson (1834–1921), pre-eminent Edinburgh architect of the day, without castle turrets or crowsteps, in the form of a sculpture-encrusted medieval Italian palazzo. Overt Baronial rhetoric was now reserved for works of public sculpture, such as William Grant Stevenson's giant statue of Wallace in the centre of Aberdeen, which portrayed the

113 National Wallace Monument, near Stirling, by J. T. Rochead, built in 1861–69: exhibition drawing of Rochead's winning entry in a national architectural competition of 1859. The immense craggy tower is set on the wooded Abbey Craig hill; it contains four vaulted halls one above another, and is capped by a crown spire. The plinth set in the south-west corner of the tower now holds a larger-than-life bronze statue of Wallace by D. W. Stevenson of 1887.

114 Scottish National Portrait Gallery, Edinburgh, by R. Rowand Anderson, 1884–89. The gabled main entrance leads into an arcaded central hall that generally recalls the Doges' Palace in Venice. The lavish sculpture, containing subjects symbolic of Scottish history, was executed by W. Birnie Rhind in 1892–93. Like Anderson's contemporary work at Mount Stuart (ill. 159), the building is faced in red Dumfriesshire sandstone.

115 Rosemount Viaduct, Aberdeen, seen in 1892 following completion of an extensive City Improvement scheme. From left to right: statue of Wallace (W. Grant Stevenson, 1888); Public Library (Brown & Watt, 1891–92); the domed South United Free Church (J. Marshall Mackenzie, 1892); and His Majesty's Theatre (Frank Matcham, 1904–8).

hero gesturing with 'mingled expressions of contempt, magnanimity, and defiance' atop a mound of 'massive rough blocks of Corrennie granite' [115]. Unveiling the statue in 1888, the Marquis of Lorne hailed Wallace as a precursor of British imperialism, concluding that 'patriotism is not proved by the loudest crowing on the nearest mound, but in the strength by which eagles claim as their eyrie the rock which is the loftiest'.

Religious Architectures

From the 1830s, the emergence of Scotch Baronial as a secular national style paralleled the growing religious associations of Gothic, especially in Edinburgh. But the results, in the main built for Presbyterian factions, were very different from the products of the English Gothic Revival, with its focus on liturgy and the decorative arts. The political rivalries of the era, above all the 1843 Disruption of the Kirk over the issue of state control of patronage, meant that most attention was devoted to the claims to national status of the rival denominations, expressed through the building of new churches. At the same time, Presbyterian ideals of personal struggle strongly infused the entire work of many important architects, such as Thomson. All in all, secular and religious architecture remained as intertwined as they had been ever since the 15th century.

This 'political' and 'secular' aspect of Scottish religious architecture emerged particularly strongly in a monumental ensemble developed over nearly four decades on the Mound in Edinburgh, at the interface of the Old and New Towns [116]. At the New Town end of the group are two secular institutions in a stately columned Grecian style by Playfair: the Royal Institution (1822–26, extended 1832–35) and the National Gallery of Scotland (1850–58) [111]. Above, in axial alignment, rise a cluster of Gothic steeples, signalling not churches but two competing Presbyterian institutional complexes. In front, overlooking the Gallery, and designed by the same architect, Playfair, is the towered façade of the college (1846–50) and national assembly hall [111] built by the Free Church – the middle-class, Liberal denomination that had seceded in 1843. Behind, its tall spire in effect appropriated by Playfair's towers, stands the Victoria Hall, built in 1839–44 as the national assembly hall for the pre-Disruption church, to the designs of James Gillespie Graham; ironically, its detail was provided by the pioneering English Gothic Revivalist, and passionate Catholic, A. W. N. Pugin (1812–52).

Immediately following the Disruption, large numbers of standard preaching-churches clad in spiky Gothic detail were built

116 'Romantic Classical' Edinburgh: late 19th-century view of Hanover Street and the Mound from the north. At the centre of the view is the Royal Institution (now the Royal Scottish Academy) by W. H. Playfair, 1822–35. Behind, clinging to the escarpment of the Old Town, are the Gothic towers of the same architect's Free Church College, 1846–50. They frame the spire of the Victoria Hall, by J. Gillespie Graham with A. W. N. Pugin, 1839–44.

117 Barclay Free Church,
Edinburgh, by F. T. Pilkington,
begun in 1861.

118 College of the Holy Spirit,
Cumbrae, by William Butterfield,
1849–51: perspective of 1852 by
Samuel Bough. Founded as a model
theological college by the fervently
Anglican 6th Earl of Glasgow, it
includes as well as the church a
chapter house and collegiate block
(on the right in this view) with
cloister behind.

– an approach exported to the colonies by Scottish architects, in locations such as the Free Church's Otago Settlement, New Zealand (from the late 1840s) [195]. By the 1860s, however, the Free Church became more experimental in its designs. Frederick T. Pilkington (1832–98) built an idiosyncratic series of Gothic churches, including what was at the time the tallest building in Scotland, commissioned in 1861 by Edinburgh's most active evangelical congregation: the Barclay Church [117], a centralized auditorium clad in a ferociously incised Gothic from Normandy and crowned by a steeple 80 metres (260 feet) high. The United Presbyterians, a church rooted especially in the intellectual classes, commissioned both classical auditoria and vigorous Gothic works, such as the roomy Camphill Church, Glasgow (1875–83), designed by William Leiper (1839–1916), with a soaring spire based on close study of St Pierre, Caen.

It was only in the minority Episcopal Church, with its Anglican liturgy, that close links with the English Gothic Revival were cultivated, and several works by front-rank English designers were built in Scotland – otherwise a rare event. William Butterfield (1814–1900), favoured architect of the high-church Ecclesiological Society, built two major Episcopal churches in 1849–51, at the College of the Holy Spirit on the Isle of Cumbrae [118], and St Ninian's Cathedral, Perth. Both fulfilled the ritualistic demands of the Society, and Pugin's picturesque and 'archaeological' principles,

with their tall naves, steep roofs, and (at Cumbrae) lofty spire. The grandest Episcopal commission of the mid- and late 19th century was the new cathedral of St Mary in Edinburgh, financed out of the profits of the western New Town development [119]. An 1872 competition was won by Sir George Gilbert Scott (1811–78), with a centralized, single-spire design, incorporating Scottish medieval detailing – subsequently modified by Scott with two western spires (built after his death, to his designs, in 1913–17).

The position of religious architecture in Glasgow was different. While there were many Gothic churches in the city, the dominant strain of church design was classical, and integrated with the Grecian/Italian styles preferred for secular architecture in the west of Scotland. The Glasgow Free Church College (1856–61) is, like Playfair's in Edinburgh [116], a towered group on a height [1, 120]; but Charles Wilson (1810–63), one of Glasgow's foremost classical architects, chose for it not Gothic but a round-arched style combining Romanesque, Quattrocento and high Renaissance. The most popular pattern for churches was a Greek temple, seen most straightforwardly at the Greek Ionic Elgin Place Congregational Church of 1855–56 by John Burnet (1814–1901). We shall turn below to the more original solutions devised by Alexander Thomson.

Architecture in the Country

Rural architecture in the 19th century was essentially similar throughout Scotland. Even at the everyday level, in buildings such as farms and cottages, vernacular regional variations were of little importance. And the grander estate buildings and country houses were built mainly by architects with nationwide practices. In the process, the Scottish roots of the landed classes and the monarchy were emphasized. That connection was expressed most tellingly in two successive projects: Taymouth Castle and Balmoral Castle. At Taymouth, William Adam's classical scheme of the 1730s [81] was largely obliterated in a neo-Gothic reconstruction project of 1806–10 by two Edinburgh architects, Archibald Elliot (1760–1823) and his brother James (1770–1810), and internally fitted out in the delicate Gothic plasterwork of the time by the

London specialist Francis Bernasconi, including a vertiginous staircase tower [123]; a further remodelling by James Gillespie Graham after 1834 provided even more sumptuous Gothic interiors in rooms such as the Library and Banner Hall.

Taymouth was visited in 1842 by Queen Victoria as the climax of her first tour of the Highlands, and it inspired her to acquire and reconstruct a castle of her own, at Balmoral in Aberdeenshire [121]. Built in 1853–56, the new Balmoral, financed out of a £500,000 bequest from a wealthy private admirer, John Camden Nield, was designed in the traditional way by a laird–architect – in this case Prince Albert, assisted by the Aberdeen City Architect William Smith (1817–91). It comprises a main block and a service block, both around courtyards, with a keep-like tower at the intersection, and a tall ballroom wing partly concealing the service block.

The style of Balmoral, unlike that of Taymouth, is not Gothic but Scotch Baronial, which had become the preferred mode for Scottish country houses by the 1850s. However, that ascendancy had taken some decades to establish, and it is worth retracing our steps a little to summarize that process. The last, greatest country house in the grand classical style was Hamilton Palace [122], enlarged in 1822–26 by the autocratic 10th Duke of Hamilton as a monumental frame for his art collection, financed by his lucrative coal-mines (and demolished in the 1920s after the exhaustion of those mines). In a joint scheme by the Glasgow architect David Hamilton (1768–1843) and various overseas consultants, the orientation was reversed [cf. 69] and a new entrance block built on the north. A lofty Corinthian portico and great cubic entrance hall led to a sequence of interiors, culminating in a circular toplit tribune. These could have been in St Petersburg or Paris,

123 Taymouth Castle, Perthshire: the staircase hall, by Archibald and James Elliot with the decorator Francis Bernasconi, 1806–10. After Lord Breadalbane had received Queen Victoria there in 1842, she recorded that 'it was as if a great chieftain in olden feudal times was receiving his sovereign. It was princely and romantic.'

124 Abbotsford, Roxburghshire, by Sir Walter Scott with William Atkinson, 1817–23: the entrance hall. The internal decoration, complete with antique furniture and armour, was organized for Scott by the renowned Edinburgh housepainter D. R. Hay.

with their overweening scale and dark marble, stone and mahogany finishes.

By the 1830s, landowners were rejecting this grand formality for a more picturesque approach. They wanted not just classical houses in Gothic dress, but houses comprehensively replanned to separate private and public apartments in a modern way. At first, the response was a 'Tudor' or 'Jacobean' manner, or an asymmetrical 'rustic Italian' classicism, but gradually the castellated Baronial became dominant. This style had already been pioneered at Abbotsford in Roxburghshire, the rural villa-retreat created in the Borders by Sir Walter Scott in 1817–23. Scott and his architect, William Atkinson (c. 1773–1839) – ironically, an Englishman – rebuilt an old farmhouse into a rambling shrine of Scottish antiquarianism, bursting with historical relics [124]

and old furniture, and externally styled in a combination of Jacobean and Adam Castle Style. The emotional impact of Scott's novels and of Abbotsford was given more scholarly flesh after 1844, with the publication of R. W. Billings's *Baronial and Ecclesiastical Antiquities of Scotland*.

During the 1830s and 1840s, William Burn (1789–1870) built numbers of houses which anticipated the general spirit, although not yet the detail, of the Scotch Baronial, combining an externally picturesque style with practical, logically planned interiors. The culmination of this spiky romanticism was designed not by Burn but by the English architect Sir Charles Barry (1795–1860), for the 2nd Duke of Sutherland: the massive enlargement of Dunrobin Castle from 1844 [128]. Working with the Aberdeen architect William Leslie (1802–79) and the Duke himself, Barry enveloped the original house in a looming, turreted crescent of apartments, including a royal reception suite. Balmoral [121], with its strong Tudor elements, is an example of this second phase of Baronial, but by the time it was built, in the 1850s, a new and far more vigorous type of Baronial was being devised by David Bryce (1803–76), who had been Burn's partner from 1841 to 1850. Bryce combined accurate quotations culled from Billings with bolder massing, to produce some of the most accomplished examples of mid-Victorian modern eclecticism. In his new or enlarged Scotch Baronial houses, culminating in Craigends, Renfrewshire (1857–59) [127], and Ballikinrain, Stirlingshire (1864–70), Bryce marshalled a variety of monumental features from Scottish Renaissance castles such as Fyvie [60] and Castle Fraser with a power and refinement quite distinct from the originals. Even the basic materials are different: sharp stonework and plate-glass windows rather than harling, rubble, and small-paned openings. A more formal, symmetrical variant of this style is 'Franco-Baronial', similar to the contemporary Second Empire style in its high roofs, turrets, and French Renaissance detailing.

The grandeur and modernity of these country seats reflected the booming Lowland rural economy. From around the 1830s until the 1870s, the buildings of the original phase of Improvement were swept away by new steading complexes, planned on openly industrial lines, embracing steam motive power and all the systems of mid-Victorian 'High Farming' behind plain Baronial frontages. Patrons and designers were spurred on by popular books such as J. C. Loudon's *Encyclopaedia of Cottage, Farm and Villa Architecture and Furniture* (London, 1833, with revised editions from 1842 onwards) [125]. At the hands of Burn and land agents such as

125 Two farm steadings, constructed on rational Improvement lines in the best quality rubble masonry, featured in J. C. Loudon's *Encyclopaedia of Cottage, Farm and Villa Architecture and Furniture*, 1833. Above: Greendykes, East Lothian, of 1832, was an arable farm planned by a Mr Swinton for David Anderson of St Germains, in a simplified Baronial style; the engine house, with chimney, is at the upper left. Greendykes was described in the *New Statistical Account* as 'more like the offices you might expect to find connected with a Ducal palace than the house of a tenant'.
Below: Elcho Castle Farm, Perthshire, a steading and detached farmhouse designed by William Mackenzie, *c.* 1830. The design, which included the novel feature of a circular feeding-house for cattle, was based on a model plan selected by the Highland Society of Scotland; Loudon praised Mackenzie as 'a thinking and ingenious man, really intent on carrying improvement into every department of his profession'.

XXXIV.

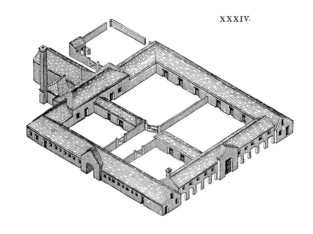

XXXV.

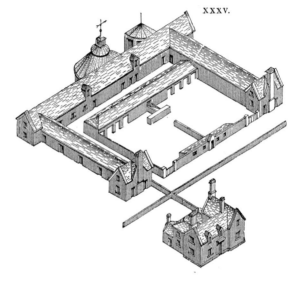

126 Skelbo Farm, 1853, a showpiece of the Duke of Sutherland's improvement programme. This large coastal steading was designed by the surveyor Robert Brown, in collaboration with the estate factor James Loch. It forms a gigantic two-storeyed letter E, with single-storey covered cattle courts flanking the central arm of the E. In this view, the three two-storeyed gabled wings (left, centre and right) contain cartsheds, a turnip feed store, and miscellaneous store-rooms. The upper floor is devoted to grain storage. The six lower gables, without chimney or bellcote, front the cattle courts.

127 Craigends, Renfrewshire, by David Bryce, 1857–59: exhibition perspective.

128 Dunrobin Castle, Sutherland, enlarged from 1844 by Sir Charles Barry with William Leslie for the 2nd Duke of Sutherland. The skyline was even more dramatically spiky before a fire in the early 20th century.

J. Young Macvicar, the Scottish pattern of rectilinear, *tabula rasa* industrial steading was also built in parts of England: for example, on Christopher Turner's estates in Lincolnshire (1840s–70s). At the same time, there were further attempts to extend Improvement across the Highlands. Above all, the dukes of Sutherland spent prodigiously on vast agricultural remodelling schemes, alongside their 'clearances' of subsistence farmers. They attempted huge wilderness reclamations and laid out extensive arable farms along the coast, such as Skelbo (1853) [126], with its E-shaped plan, covered cattle courts, and array of nine crowstepped gables.

Across rural Scotland, Scotch Baronial became the style of preference for public buildings. And in an offshoot of the international grand hotel movement, new hydropathic institutions and hotels sprang up in railway towns ringing the Highlands. The greatest was the Atholl Palace Hotel at Pitlochry, Perthshire, designed by the Perth architect Andrew Heiton (1823–94) and

129 Atholl Palace Hotel, Pitlochry, Perthshire, by Andrew Heiton, 1875–78, photographed when newly completed.

built at the enormous cost of £100,000 [129]; the domineering H-planned, towered Franco-Baronial block was finished in rustic rock-faced masonry, and overlooked steep alpine landscaping.

Architecture in City and Town

For all the wealth of the countryside, it was the explosive growth of the cities that dominated 19th-century Scottish architecture. There was civic and capitalist confidence in plenty, but at the same time there was a mounting sense of crisis, moral, social and medical, which provoked a range of religious and secular reformist proposals. For this crisis was not just a matter for the slums, but equally struck at the middle classes, including architects. For example, Alexander Thomson lost three out of his first four children to the 1854 cholera epidemic, before the family moved away from their Gorbals house to an outer suburb of Glasgow.

Architectural responses to the crisis fell into two main groups: those that set out to remedy it, through utopian or pragmatic policies; and those that tried to escape it, especially by creating a new sphere of the 'domestic'. The most extreme of the reformist solutions were those of the utopians – above all Robert Owen, the Welsh cotton-master who took over the New Lanark settlement in 1800 and began to develop it on communitarian lines [98]. From the 1820s, with American collaborators,

Owen developed a succession of radical proposals for new agro-industrial communities, including enclosed residential blocks with central schools and communal dining rooms. Although unrealized, these ideas prefigured some of the 20th century's concepts of zoning and planned settlements.

The mainstream of reformism concentrated on what could be done within existing towns and civic institutions: utopia should be built at home. The governing ethos was a mixture of Liberal civic pride and evangelical, Masonic Presbyterianism. An enabling framework for suburban growth was provided by a combination of private and civic regulation, and for slum redevelopment by a succession of Improvement Acts. The escapist retreat from the public to the domestic was bound up with the growing prestige of the detached house and the separate suburb, although most new suburban dwellings continued to be built in the form of tenement blocks of flats, without any suggestion of a general stigma attaching to the type. This tenement tradition was part of a wider European norm of flatted urban housing – in contrast to the compressed row-houses of England and Wales – but the use of 'perimeter' street layouts (with large communal back courts), 'terraced' façade repetition, and industrial materials and techniques, were all closer to the English pattern. The combination of radical surgery in the old centres, and new, segregated domestic suburbs, was influenced by the colonial planning principles pioneered in India by Scots such as the hygienist Sir John Ritchie Simpson and the military engineer Lord Napier of Magdala. In the wake of the 1857 'Indian Mutiny', Napier opened up wide boulevards through the old towns of Delhi and Lucknow, and laid out segregated 'cantonments' for European residents.

These conflicting trends of dispersal and transformation were reconciled by a continuing recognition that the city was a single entity, whose ordered street layouts, parks and public buildings could combine the pursuit of responsible citizenship and the private universe. Yet there was also a strong regional distinctiveness among these emerging urban architectures, especially between Glasgow and Edinburgh – even as the old vernacular diversity of pre-Improvement rural Scotland disappeared. The specialized city institutions were supported by a range of specific building types, differentiated by variations of classical eclecticism. The rising demand for capital from the 1820s, for example, stimulated the building of large numbers of bank chambers, containing grand halls, offices and vaults, and designed

130 Aberdeen New Market, by Archibald Simpson, 1840–42: the galleried interior, over 100 metres (some 300 feet) long, included broad aisles with rows of shops on either side of the vast central space. It was demolished in the 1960s.

by company consultant architects in styles to suit location and status: the most important of the Commercial Bank's commissions to David Rhind (1808–83), the Edinburgh headquarters of 1843 and the Glasgow branch of 1853–57, were designed respectively as a Corinthian-porticoed temple and a Renaissance palazzo. The emergence of an architecture of consumer consumption and 'leisure space' prompted different classical permutations. The Aberdeen New Market of 1840–42 [130] by Archibald Simpson (1790–1847) pioneered the attempt to create a more substantial and prestigious setting for market shops and stalls, by combining an austere anta-order façade with a galleried interior redolent of the cella of a temple.

Glasgow and the West

As one of the most advanced capitalist cities of the mid-19th century, Glasgow developed a highly differentiated structure, with a constellation of suburbs around a constantly redeveloping public centre. An American visitor in the 1840s remarked that Glasgow was 'one continuous building site'. By 1912, the city's municipal territory was ten times larger than that of 1830. During the early 19th century, Glasgow's commercial élite had evolved a laissez-faire culture of opulent display, with domestic interiors for show rather than for privacy. But the growing public-health crisis provoked its evangelical rulers to sweeping measures of public intervention, beginning with the 1855–59 project, opened by Queen Victoria, to draw city water from Loch Katrine, enlisting the romantic purity of the Highlands to help regenerate the corrupted city. The middle classes sought escape in a variety of picturesque and sinuously planned suburbs. Some of these were reached by a new, arrow-straight artery to the north-west, Great Western Road (laid out in 1836), flanked by a succession of terraces. One, Grosvenor Terrace of 1855 [131], was designed by J. T. Rochead, the architect of the Wallace Monument [113], and featured an extraordinarily uniform Venetian-arched frontage. In the south-side suburb of West Pollokshields, laid out in 1849 by David Rhind, the emphasis was entirely on detached villas in leafy grounds – a form of development which also spread to high-class resorts along the nearby Clyde coast, such as Helensburgh, the location of numerous villas by William Leiper (1839–1916) and other key Glasgow designers. Within the old centre, a City

131 Grosvenor Terrace, Great Western Road, Glasgow, by J. T. Rochead, 1855.

Improvement Trust was set up in 1866, to tear down and redevelop the worst slums of the inner city with wide boulevards modelled on Haussmann's Paris. After the Education Act of 1872, the initiative in social building passed to the school boards around the city. But increasingly it was Glasgow Corporation that orchestrated the public interest, developing its multifarious activities into a comprehensive 'municipal socialism'.

The energy of Glasgow's civic life was mirrored in its architectural world. Up until the 1840s, the demands of its élite classes for new banks, clubs and dwellings were met mainly through a florid classicism, mingling elements from Greece and the Italian Renaissance with other styles: unusually, Glasgow's more full-blooded 19th-century eclecticism did not reject the Grecian style, but restrained and modified it. This approach was foreshadowed in the work of Stark, but it was David Hamilton who pioneered the new urban eclecticism in the 1820s, doubtless under the influence of his Hamilton Palace work. At the new Royal Exchange (1827–29), he expressed the collective life of the city's mercantile classes through a heavy, Corinthian-porticoed enlargement of an 18th-century mansion, crowned by a stubby tower. The Exchange occupies an important axial position, and a new square by Hamilton and his son-in-law James Smith (1808–63)

132 22 Park Circus, Glasgow: cast-iron dome over the staircase hall, by James Boucher, 1872–74. This sumptuous house, commissioned by the iron manufacturer and exporter Walter Macfarlane, was built externally in conformity with the sober Renaissance formula laid down in 1854 by Charles Wilson. Internally, however, it presented a sequence of overpoweringly ornate rooms, culminating in a galleried upper staircase hall with scalloped and glazed dome made at Macfarlane's Saracen Ironworks. A later scheme of lavish Art Nouveau decoration was overlaid on Boucher's interiors in 1897–99 by James Salmon and John Gaff Gillespie.

was built around it in 1830–39. Hamilton's Western Club (1840) is a vast palazzo with end bays punctuated by triple windows in pilastered settings, like Venetian windows turned rectilinear – a forerunner of the trabeated style that was to be so important to Alexander Thomson. Hamilton's main follower, Charles Wilson, vigorously developed the theme of mixed Italian and Greek classicism. Like contemporaries in Germany, he evolved a round-arched amalgam of Romanesque and Renaissance with a somewhat Quattrocento air. Wilson's most important city-centre commission was his Venetian-arched Royal Faculty of Procurators building of 1854. His key works are concentrated in the city's residential West End. The spindly round-arched towers of his Free Church College [120] crown the imposing Woodlands Hill development (from 1855), with its highly variegated curving classical terraces [1]. These include Wilson's own Park Circus, an introverted space with stately part-rusticated façades, and the more assertive, bay-windowed French Renaissance of Park Terrace, commanding the public outlook over Kelvingrove Park. The interiors of these grand houses were often designed as separate projects by other architects, showcasing the innovative materials and assembly techniques of Glasgow's industrial and (later) shipbuilding complex: for example, James Boucher (1832–92) drew up a lavish classical scheme for the iron manufacturer Walter Macfarlane at 22 Park Circus (1872–74), making every possible use of metal [132]. Just to the south of Woodlands Hill, Wilson designed the equally sumptuous Queen's Rooms (1857–58), a public hall richly endowed by a prominent Glasgow merchant. Its Renaissance round-arched façades were crammed with sculpture (by John Mossman) allegorical of Glasgow's civic, masonic and imperial patriotism.

Glasgow's complex world of Grecian eclecticism was dominated by the architecture of Alexander Thomson – indeed, he was nicknamed 'Greek' Thomson. Driven by a Presbyterian zeal for betterment and redemption, yet set apart by his reputation as an idealistic dreamer, Thomson set out to create an eclectic classical style which could represent the numinous and the eternal, while serving the practical demands of collective urban life. Along with his stylistic opponents, the English Gothic Revival designers, he formed part of the mid-19th-century movement in Britain and America to devise personal or free styles, whose emotional intensity, subjectivity and integrity would set them apart from the mundane world of 'correct' historical ornament – an outlook that presaged some important aspects of the 'modern' architectures of the 20th century.

133 Caledonia Road United Presbyterian Church, Glasgow, by Alexander Thomson, 1856–57. The galleried church is at ground level, with the portico perched above the entrance hall for purely architectural effect. The tenement on the right was built by the congregation to Thomson's designs as a speculative investment. (Shortly after 1964, when this photograph was taken, the church was gutted by fire; the tenement was subsequently demolished.)

Thomson designed a mixture of churches [133 – 135], commercial buildings [137] and housing (including numerous tenement blocks) [133, 136], almost all in a forceful Greek style with idiosyncratic elements culled from the illustrated source-books of the day – including, for instance, the published works of the Prussian architect Karl Friedrich Schinkel (1781–1841). In his churches and villas, he combined elements of horizontal repetition (emphasized by Schinkel-style lines of inset rectangular piers) with massively emphatic vertical punctuations, within an overall aesthetic of the monumental Sublime, and detailed on the whole with incised rather than 'add-on' ornament. His three most

134 St Vincent Street United Presyterian Church, Glasgow, by Alexander Thomson, 1857–59. In this design, arguably the greatest work of 19th-century Scottish architecture, Thomson brilliantly exploited the sharply sloping site to realize his vision of a modern 'Temple of Solomon'. The auditorium is sunk deep into the massive podium, above which rise the temple superstructure and the fantastically ornamented tower.

135 St Vincent Street United Presyterian Church, Glasgow: the interior seen from the entrance at street level at the top of the site.

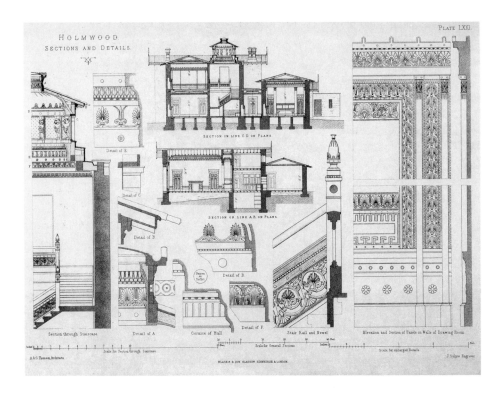

PLATE LXXI.

HOLMWOOD
SECTIONS AND DETAILS.

SECTION ON LINE C D ON PLANS.

Detail of E.

Detail of G

SECTION ON LINE A B ON PLANS.

Detail of B

Detail of D.

Section through Staircase.   Detail of A.   Cornice of Hall.   Detail of F.   Stair Rail and Newel.   Elevation and Section of Panels on Walls of Drawing Room.

Scale for Section through Staircase.   Scale for General Sections.   Scale for enlarged Details.

A. & G. Thomson, Architects.   BLACKIE & SON, GLASGOW, EDINBURGH & LONDON.   J. Sulpis Engraver.

136 Alexander Thomson: sections and interior details of Holmwood, near Glasgow, 1857–58, from *Villa and Cottage Architecture*, 1868. This plate illustrates the highly unified and architectonic decorative vocabulary synthesized by Thomson out of a wide range of eclectic sources. The somewhat repetitive geometrical motifs lent themselves to machine-aided assembly techniques, exploiting the technology of a shipbuilding industrial city.

important churches, Caledonia Road (1856–57), St Vincent Street (1857–59), and the war-destroyed Queen's Park (1867–69), all built for the United Presbyterian Church, integrated galleried auditorium plans within a pyramidal massing of interpenetrating blocks, intended to evoke the Temple of Solomon; internally, there was an increasingly ambitious use of polychromatic stencilled decoration [135]. At Caledonia Road, the overall style is still relatively restrained and neoclassical [133]. The pilastered auditorium block is juxtaposed with an Ionic portico, raised on a podium, and a tall, rectangular steeple of Early Christian character (recalling that of St Rule's Church at St Andrews [18]). St Vincent Street, whose scheme was complicated by the addition of galleried aisles, was built on a sloping site, allowing the church to be sunk into a massive base, punched with window-bands [134]. The taller central section rises above in temple form and the campanile-like steeple, its upper stages ornamented with Egyptian motifs, stands at the side. The Middle-Eastern theme was expanded at Queen's Park, which resembled Caledonia Road in its plinth and portico formula, but was crowned by a pylon and squat dome. Although the interpenetrating lines of pilasters and columns were retained, the style was no longer specifically Grecian. Inside, Thomson worked with the artist Daniel Cottier (1838–91), using for the stencilwork soft 'tertiary' colours, in anticipation of the Aesthetic Movement, while retaining the machine-assembly sharpness of the Glasgow interior-decorative tradition.

A similar combination of picturesque towered asymmetry and Sublime massiveness, with highly 'architectural' polychromatic interior schemes designed by the architect, characterized Thomson's detached villas, such as Holmwood, south of Glasgow (1857–58) [136], commissioned by a wealthy mill-owner. Holmwood's heroic classical interior decoration included a dining room frieze reproducing Flaxman's illustrations of the *Iliad*, and drawing-room paintings by Hugh Cameron, inspired by Tennyson's 'Idylls of the King'.

Thomson's urban commercial and domestic work was different in character, as it had to fit into tightly confined street façades and plots. Here a towered asymmetry was obviously inappropriate, and he instead emphasized the unifying effect of repetitive horizontal elements, using concealed iron reinforcement to permit long bands of windows and piers to be sunk into the wall-plane. Instead of the academic orders to differentiate the various storeys, he used more exotic eclectic devices. At the Egyptian Halls (1871–73) [137], a four-storey commercial block in central Glasgow, a traditional palazzo form

137 Egyptian Halls, Glasgow, by Alexander Thomson, 1871–73. The original shopfronts had unifying outer bands around plate-glass windows; the shop second from left is in close to original condition.

138 Govanhill School, Glasgow, by H. & D. Barclay, 1886–87.

was transformed into a vertical stack of glass shop-fronts and pilastered and colonnaded upper storeys. In Thomson's urban housing designs, the same principles applied: the conventional classical differentiation of the various storeys was replaced by a freer approach. For tenements [133], a highly repetitive, low-relief incised style was most usual, while in the most stately contexts, an austere treatment redolent of Grecian neoclassicism might still be appropriate: in 1–10 Moray Place (from 1859), a row of houses including Thomson's own home, he linked pedimented outer pavilions with a ruthlessly uniform range of closely pilastered bays, while at Great Western Terrace (from 1869) he set two palazzo-like blocks within a severe two-storey range, the whole marked only by austere colonnaded entrances to the individual houses.

All in all, Thomson's work should be seen as a part of the High Victorian 'neo-Sublime', with its love of massiveness, but his horizontal rhythms and incised surface patterning gave his buildings a unity no English High Victorian work achieved. More comparable was the slightly later work of H. H. Richardson (1838–86) in the United States; although any direct link between the two has yet to be established, Daniel Cottier's work in America from the early 1870s may have provided a connection. In Glasgow, the main legacy of Thomson's work, after his death in 1875, was to legitimize Greek classicism as the continuing mainstream of the city's architecture. His most immediate follower was James Sellars (1843–88), whose early works in the 1870s developed Thomsonian themes of grand colonnaded and interpenetrating temple forms, for example at Kelvinside Academy (1877) or in the gigantic block of St Andrew's Hall (1873–77), whose galleried auditorium (later destroyed by fire) was fronted by a giant Ionic colonnade and caryatid attic pavilions. In the work of Hugh Barclay (1828–92) and his brother David (1846–1917), prolific designers of board schools across Clydeside in the 1870s and 1880s (following the passing of the 1872 Education Act), the influence of Thomson was extended to the emergent field of social building, and mingled with Renaissance classicism. For instance, Jean Street School in Port Glasgow (1883) takes the form of a square palazzo with Thomson window-bands on all three floors, while the slightly later Govanhill School in Glasgow (1886–87) [138] is more explicitly Italian in style, acknowledging Thomson only in the grouped upper-floor fenestration.

Edinburgh, Aberdeen and the East
The architectural culture of the two main east coast urban centres, Edinburgh and Aberdeen, developed on different and more conservative lines. In Edinburgh, the growth of the city occurred in

139 Moray Place, Edinburgh, by J. Gillespie Graham, 1822–36. The twelve-sided open space is ringed by stepped ranks of giant orders, arranged in the now-established palace-front manner (cf. ill. 104). The composition is ingeniously varied to accommodate an irregular pattern of side streets, which requires two of the sides (including the one illustrated here) to be much longer than the others.

140 Signet (Upper) Library, Edinburgh Law Courts, by William Stark, after 1812. With its complex nave-and-aisles arrangement and central dome, this was a harbinger of the richer classicism of such mid-century designs as the University Library by Stark's pupil Playfair. Appropriately, in Edinburgh's classical Enlightenment, the most monumental interiors were those of libraries.

two sharply differentiated phases. Hectic expansion in 1800–1830, which saw a doubling of the population, was focused on realizing the idea of the city as the 'Modern Athens' through completion of the New Town. It was brought to an end by the bankruptcy of the town council. When residential development resumed from the 1850s, the preferred image was that of the romantic, pre-classical Old Edinburgh of Walter Scott.

The years after 1810 saw the 'Grecianizing' of the New Town. New developments took the form of often astylar terraces and tenements interspersed with monumental public buildings – all following a restrained neoclassical eclecticism which perpetuated Robert Adam's philosophy of 'movement'. In the 1810s Stark and Playfair attacked the uniformity of the first New Town façades, and advocated more variegated layouts of terraces and greenery, inspired generally by the work of John Nash (1752–1835) in London. This call was first answered in Archibald Elliot's Grecian Waterloo Place of 1815–22, with the crags of Calton Hill looming up behind its flanking porticoes and arcaded viaduct (spanning an earlier road far below, in the manner of the South Bridge); and it found its most monumental realization in the ponderous façades designed by James Gillespie Graham for the Earl of Moray's Drumsheugh Estate from 1822 [139].

The most prestigious projects of the period were designed by the three leaders of Edinburgh neoclassicism: William Henry Playfair, William Burn and Thomas Hamilton. Playfair, a pupil of Stark and a favourite of the city's Whig and Free Church intellectuals, specialized in the scholarly design of public buildings, and condemned the florid richness of Glasgow architects such as David Hamilton as ostentatious and vulgar. Playfair's townscape masterpiece is the classical and Gothic ensemble on the Mound [111, 116], and his noblest interior the pilastered and Ionic-screened University Upper Library (part of his extensive 1819–27 work to complete Adam's quadrangle project), but he also contributed numerous other monumental punctuations to the capital's streets. These included the temple-porticoed Surgeons' Hall (1829–32) and St Stephen's Church (1827–28) [141], terminating an axial street with its oversized pilastered entrance tower and chunky

141 St Stephen's Church, Edinburgh, by W. H. Playfair, 1827–28.

142 British Linen Bank, St Andrew Square, Edinburgh, by David Bryce, 1846–51. The arrangement of the thrust-forward, statue-supporting columns is ancient Roman in origin, like the motif in Robert Adam's anteroom at Syon House (ill. 89); the statues, by A. Handyside Ritchie, depict Navigation, Commerce, Manufacture, Science, Art and Agriculture.

143 Bank of Scotland, Edinburgh, by David Bryce, 1864–70: perspective showing St Giles's and the Old Town as a romantic backdrop (for the finished building in context, see ill. 111). This project was a reconstruction and enlargement of Robert Reid and William Crichton's original building of 1801–6.

144 Fettes College, Edinburgh, by David Bryce, 1864–70. It is an indication of Bryce's eclectic skill that he could work on two such monumental commissions, in strikingly different styles, at the same time.

finials. In his designs for the New Town extension around Calton Hill, Playfair maintained an uncompromising urban grandeur, whose climax was the palace-like façade of Royal Terrace, built from 1821, with its hierarchy of colonnades. Burn, in addition to his growing national country-house clientèle, also maintained a more localized Edinburgh urban workload of public buildings and housing, including the low, porticoed group of the Edinburgh Academy (1822–24); the move towards Italian models was demonstrated in his sober palazzo for the New Club (1834). Hamilton's œuvre, although much smaller, included the Royal High School [112], prominent through its Calton Hill site, and the Royal College of Physicians, with its Grecian portico surmounted by a Hellenistic aedicule, flanked by lifesize statues (1844–46).

By the 1840s and 1850s, the curtailment of the New Town brought new types of development to prominence. What was demanded now was not so much collective urban environments as institutions for the financial and cultural élites, designed in a more individually assertive way: between 1850 and 1914, almost a thousand new civic, public and religious buildings were constructed in Edinburgh. The emblematic type of the mid-century was the large private school [144], bristling with towers like a Baronial house, but symmetrical like Heriot's [51]: the pioneer was Playfair's Elizabethan palace design for Donaldson's Hospital (a philanthropic school for the deaf), built in 1842–50. The capital's new architectural leader was David Bryce, who

145 Life Association of Scotland, Princes Street, Edinburgh, by David Rhind, 1855–58, photographed just prior to its demolition in 1967.

developed Burn's dual country-house/Edinburgh practice. His urban work had in common with that of his Glasgow contemporaries a forcefully modelled classical eclecticism. But Bryce's approach was in a way less free-ranging, using ancient Roman and Baroque sources within a framework of practical modernity. In his projects for banks and financial offices up to the 1870s, he designed bolder variants of the palazzo formula. The British Linen Bank in St Andrew Square (1846–51) [142] is fronted by a Baalbek-like array of colossal detached Corinthian columns, behind which rises a grand stair-hall and telling room ringed by granite monoliths, while his Franco-Italian enlargement of the Bank of Scotland headquarters on the Mound (1864–70) [111, 143] almost constitutes an artificial hill with its piling-up of rustication, columns and domes. For some urban building types, Bryce thought it more appropriate to import Scotch Baronial from the country, for use in symmetrical groups: for example, in his turreted, pavilioned Edinburgh Royal Infirmary (from 1872), or in the palatial, spired Franco-Baronial of Fettes College, a private school (1864–70) [144]. The work of David Rhind in Edinburgh also illustrated the trend towards a richer Renaissance classicism, leaving behind the porticoed clarity of his 1843 Commercial Bank headquarters for the overpoweringly ornate Venetian Renaissance confection of the Life Association building

(1855–58) [145] – situated right next door to Burn's chaste New Club of 1834.

Mid-century Edinburgh architecture was strongly influenced by theories of harmonic proportioning, propagated especially by the painter D. R. Hay. The most extreme exponent of these theories was James Gowans (1821–90), quarrymaster, contractor, amateur architect, and passionate advocate of the use of stone construction for all purposes. He used his own fantastically turreted house, Rockville (1858) [146], as a laboratory for eccentric theories of modular stone patterning. A more sober rationalism, allied to the possibilities of iron construction, was seen in the projects of the government architect Robert Matheson (1808–77) – including the domed Botanic Garden Palm House (1855) and the multi-storey Renaissance General Post Office (1861–66) – and in the Royal Scottish Museum of 1860–61, designed by the English engineer Captain Francis Fowke (1823–65), with its Germanic arched Renaissance façades [191] and galleried iron hall behind.

146 Rockville, Edinburgh, by James Gowans, 1858. Gowans's own house was built in accordance with complex formulae of geometric proportion, and using a grid of 2-foot (61-cm) squares of cyclopean rubble held in ashlar bands, supposedly to allow mass-production of stone components. It too was demolished in the 1960s.

147 Looking west down Union Street, Aberdeen, in the early 20th century. The medieval heart of the city, Castle Street – the old Castlegate – is in the foreground. Union Street was laid out in 1794 by county road surveyor Charles Abercrombie and built from 1801 onwards. Principal buildings from left to right: the porticoed Union Buildings (Archibald Simpson, 1822–23); the Baronial-towered County and Municipal Buildings (Peddie & Kinnear, 1866–74); the dark spire of the surviving tolbooth (1616–30); and the curved portico of the North of Scotland Bank (Simpson, 1839–42).

The resumption of middle-class residential spread in 1850s and 1860s Edinburgh brought new villa suburbs, as well as a more highly modelled, Renaissance-influenced urban classicism for the western extensions of the New Town. But by then, emphasis had shifted to regeneration of the Old Town, in a historically attuned manner distinct from the Glasgow City Improvement schemes. As early as 1817–24, Thomas Hamilton and William Burn proposed to open more access streets to the Old Town, using bridges or embankments in the manner already pioneered in the previous century; work began in 1829, following the passing of the 1827 City Improvement Act [111]. The 1850s–70s saw further surgery on the Old Town fabric, and the formation of a Glasgow-style City Improvement Trust in 1867. The redevelopments were designed in picturesque styles to echo the spirit of the Old Town: the most elaborate was the curving, turreted design of Baronial tenements for Cockburn Street, planned in 1856 and built in 1859–64, by Peddie & Kinnear (John Dick Peddie [1824–91] and Charles Kinnear [1830–94]).

The north-eastern city of Aberdeen boasted a refined and self-contained architectural culture, fuelled by the profits of the regional farming and fishing industries [115, 130, 147]. Like Edinburgh, the city took up Grecian neoclassicism around 1815, and developed it with unswerving consistency until the early 1840s, using the local grey granite as a unifying element, and the south-western extension axis of Union Street as a city-planning stimulus

[147]. Aberdeen's two foremost architects were Archibald Simpson and John Smith (1781–1852). They strove to create a Granite City through such ensembles as King Street (1816–30), with its Grecian public buildings and Gothic churches. By 1840, Simpson, like David Hamilton in Glasgow, had evolved a richer classical manner. His most accomplished late work, the North of Scotland Bank office (1839–42), commands the city's most important intersection with a sumptuous quadrant portico [147], crowned with a statue of Ceres to symbolize the north-east's agricultural prosperity. This classical consistency was eventually broken by Aberdeen's most prominent later 19th-century public monument, the County and Municipal Buildings (1866–74), designed by the Edinburgh architects Peddie & Kinnear in a massively towered Scotch Baronial manner [147].

Late Victorian Architecture, 1880–1900

In the last two decades of the century, the east–west regional contrast diminished in intensity, mainly because of a decline in the use of ornament-loaded period styles to denote meaning and purpose in buildings. This formed part of a wider unease about the

148 Templeton carpet works, Glasgow, by William Leiper, 1882–92. On the right is the corner of an Art Deco extension of 1936 by George Boswell.

excesses of modern capitalism, questioning its mass-produced culture and ornament as false and alienating. Explicit historical–narrative styles began to be squeezed to the margins of architecture, to buildings such as factories, shops and international exhibitions, where they were reduced to an advertising function. The most gorgeously exaggerated example of this trend is William Leiper's polychromatic brick façade for the Templeton carpet works in Glasgow (1882–92) [148], its Venetian-Moorish arched style proclaiming a Near-Eastern luxury.

What began to emerge in place of the 'great styles' was a looser pattern of building-type themes, each associated with a combination of ethical and visual values. There were four especially important groupings: a grand Renaissance public architecture associated with the growing power of the state; a lavish classical commercial architecture; a monumental neo-medieval church architecture; and a domestic villa architecture inspired by 'homely' pre-Improvement values. These recipes were often in conflict with each other. Instead of the battle of the styles, there were new polarizations, notably between private and public architecture – a diversity exploited by a new generation of versatile architects, such as A. G. Sydney Mitchell (1856–1930) and R. Rowand Anderson of Edinburgh, John James Burnet (1857–1938) of Glasgow and Alexander Marshall Mackenzie (1847–1933) of Aberdeen.

This was the era when public-authority architecture began to gain greatly in scale and complexity, as the state extended tentacles into all aspects of life, in response to the external and internal stresses of imperialism and class conflict. For the moment, this was mainly achieved through an expansion of municipal programmes, which continued and accentuated the civic regionalism and diversity of 19th-century society. Architecturally, these programmes were expressed through variations on the traditional palace-style public building. The symbolic focus of this 'municipal socialism' was the new headquarters, or 'Municipal Buildings', erected by Glasgow Corporation in 1883–88 in George Square [149–151]. Designed by William Young (1843–1900), the gigantic classical pile contains ten million bricks and hundreds of thousands of cubic feet of finely cut ashlar. It has a rectangular plan round a central courtyard, with two lavish alabaster and marble staircases ascending to the great public chambers on the first floor. This is a building as stately and sumptuous as Hamilton Palace sixty years previously, but built by the civic community rather than a plutocratic landowner. At the foundation-laying in

1883, attended by over 500,000 people, councillors lauded the 'entirely local' character of the Municipal Buildings: this was to be 'no State-aided institution, but the citizens' own, to be erected with their money, to be dedicated to their use, and to pass under their exclusive control'. Stirred by rivalry, other towns vied to build their own municipal palaces: the Clydeside shipbuilding burgh of Greenock commissioned H. & D. Barclay to design a grand headquarters in their distinctive Thomsonian Graeco-Renaissance style, complete with covered carriage drive and a domed 'Victoria Tower' 80 metres (260 feet) high (1881–89).

The same search for architectonic gravity and secular sacredness flavoured other public institutional projects of the time. In Glasgow, the architectural profession looked to the French Beaux-Arts system as a way of giving monumental buildings a more rational and consistent character. A succession of young architects, led by J. J. Burnet in 1875–77, made the pilgrimage to the *atelier* of J. L. Pascal in Paris. On his return, Burnet designed a series of chaste modern classical institutional buildings with a marked Greek flavour, including the Royal Glasgow Fine Art Institute of 1878. In Edinburgh and the east, a new generation of designers adapted the Bryce tradition of Italian classicism for new building tasks. For example, Sydney Mitchell addressed the growing demand for modern lunatic asylum accommodation by developing a new, dispersed 'colony' layout type, with separate blocks for different types of patients, set in lavish landscaping: the first and most grandiose was the New Craighouse complex in Edinburgh (from 1889), with a massive Free Renaissance central block.

Alongside these civic-led efforts at a renewal of monumental classicism at home, Scottish architects were also involved in the search for a grand expression for British imperial power, to put London monumentally on equal terms, at last, with Paris. Here Beaux-Arts classicism was obviously an inappropriate response. The alternative, largely devised by Scottish architects resident in London, was an individualistic 'Protestant' classicism steeped in the English heritage of Inigo Jones and Christopher Wren. The Burn-trained Richard Norman Shaw (1831–1912) first signalled a return to monumental order in such works as the hybrid Baronial–classical New Scotland Yard police headquarters (1887–90). In 1889, the Dunfermline-born John M. Brydon (1840–1901) went further, arguing that the English Renaissance of Jones and Wren was 'the national style – the vernacular of the country'. In 1898, Scottish architects were awarded two

149, 150 Glasgow Municipal
Buildings, by William Young,
1883–88: plans of the main upper
floor and the ground floor, with the
main façade to the west (at the
bottom) in each case. Young's
carefully balanced plan places the
council chamber at the centre of
the main façade. The chief public
reception rooms, including the
great banqueting hall, stretch out
to the north/north-east of the
courtyard (left in the plans), and
the Lord Provost's suite and
committee rooms to the
south/south-west. The two zones
are reached by the public or
banqueting hall staircase to the
north (ill. 151), and the council
staircase to the south. (From
Young's *The Municipal Buildings,
Glasgow*, 1890)

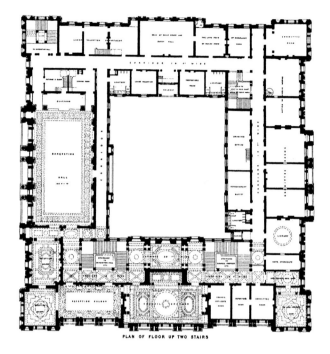

PLAN OF FLOOR UP TWO STAIRS

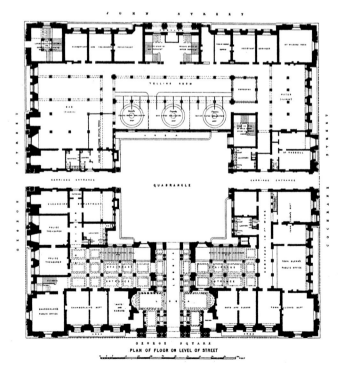

PLAN OF FLOOR ON LEVEL OF STREET

151 Glasgow Municipal Buildings:
the banqueting hall (public)
staircase. This is the more
sumptuous of the two matching
staircases, with its richly coloured
marble and alabaster panels and
columns, its ornately vaulted
ceilings, and its crowning dome.
The council staircase is dimly
visible in the distance.

152 New Government Offices,
London, by John M. Brydon, begun
in 1898: perspective of the circular
courtyard, published in *Academy
Architecture*, 1900.

153 Jenners department store,
Edinburgh, by W. Hamilton Beattie,
1893–95: illustration from a
contemporary advertisement,
which proclaimed the building's use
of 'Stuart's Granolithic Fireproof
Flooring'.

important commissions for imperial State administrative buildings. The first, designed by Brydon himself, was the New Government Offices complex in Parliament Square, a Baroque set-piece with its rusticated base and cupola-towered roofline echoing St Paul's Cathedral, and a circular court recalling the Whitehall Palace designs of Inigo Jones and John Webb [152]. The other, awarded to William Young, was a new War Office complex in Whitehall, designed to harmonize with Jones's adjacent Banqueting House.

The drive for more stately classicism made less impact in the field of commercial building. Indeed, by the 1890s, buildings such as hotels, department stores and office blocks had become a last redoubt for ornament-laden historicism. W. Hamilton Beattie (1840–98) built the most renowned examples, the North British Hotel [111] and Jenners department store [153] in Edinburgh, in

154 Waterloo Chambers, Glasgow, by J. J. Burnet, 1898–1900, seen newly completed.

1892–96 and 1893–95 respectively: the North British, with its central palm court and tall if squat-proportioned clock tower, originally contained seven hundred rooms and consumed over 1,600 tonnes of steel framing. In Glasgow, rising property values and the availability of electric power for lifts were forcing up building heights to a point where such detail-congested façades would become unsustainable. The solution, devised by Burnet and his partner, John A. Campbell (1859–1909), was to treat commercial buildings in a more unified and dynamic manner, beginning with two 1898–1900 office buildings, Atlantic and Waterloo [154] Chambers. These multi-storey blocks of lettable office space, on tight dumb-bell plans, are fronted by vigorously columned, bay-windowed and eaves-galleried façades which recall elements of the early Chicago skyscraper style. In the wake of Burnet and Campbell, other architects developed the narrow, deep plots of the central Glasgow grid with elevator-served office blocks of marked vertical proportions. The most extreme was St Vincent Chambers [155], known as the 'Hatrack', built in 1899–1902 to the designs of Salmon & Son & Gillespie (W. Forrest

155 St Vincent Chambers, Glasgow, by Salmon & Son & Gillespie, 1899–1902.

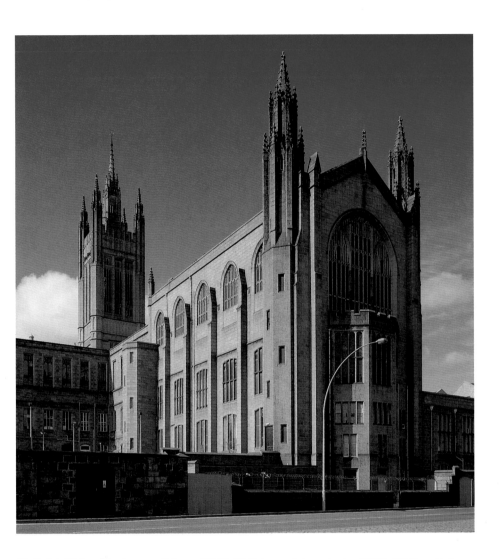

156 Marischal College Extension, Aberdeen, by Alexander Marshall Mackenzie, 1893–1903. This view shows the vast new examination hall and the Mitchell Tower. Constructed entirely from load-bearing Kemnay stone, the soaring complex is the second largest granite building in the world after the Escorial. It was hailed on its completion by one local commentator as 'a testimony to the superb durability of our Aberdeenshire granite, and the pride of our silver city by the sea'.

Salmon [1843–1911], James Salmon junior [1873–1924] and John Gaff Gillespie [1870–1926]). This slender, ten-storey office block is faced with bay windows and adorned with Art Nouveau sculpture and ironwork, its wall thickness minimized by cantilevering the floors from a double central row of columns.

In the field of church architecture, a national convergence was encouraged by liturgical and stylistic factors. Late 19th-century Presbyterianism saw the first steps towards reunification, and the rise of the 'renascence of worship' movement, advocating Episcopal-style elements of ceremony. Although the Greek temple tradition survived in Glasgow to the end of the century, in such monumental works as the Barclays' St George's-in-the-Fields (1885–86), it was finally swamped by a flood of stately Gothic Presbyterian churches, combining the Calvinistic galleried preaching auditorium with the linear plans and decorative intensity of Anglicanism. The movement began with medium-scale commissions: for instance, Anderson's Old Parish Church at Govan, Lanarkshire (1882–88), and Burnet's Barony Church, Glasgow (1886–90), with wide auditorium-naves and narrower chancels. By around 1890, endowments from rich industrialists allowed churches of cathedral scale to be started, such as the Clark Memorial Church of 1890–92 dominating the seafront at Largs, Ayrshire, by T. G. Abercrombie (1862–1926), and the crown-steepled Coats Memorial Baptist Church in Paisley, Renfrewshire, completed in 1894, by Hippolyte Blanc (1844–1917). Aberdeen witnessed a sudden outbreak of tall, spired granite churches. The most prodigious in scale was a combined university and church complex, Marischal College Extension/Greyfriars Church [156], built in 1893–1903 by Alexander Marshall Mackenzie

157 Crathie Parish Church, Aberdeenshire, by Alexander Marshall Mackenzie, 1893–95. Although also built in unyielding granite, this design contrasts strikingly in its squat simplicity with the spiny verticality of Marischal College Extension (ill. 156).

in a skyscraper-Perpendicular style, with a tall tower above the university stair-hall. An equal monumental dignity emerged in the design of some smaller churches, which emphasize a primitive heaviness, with small windows and low towers. At Mackenzie's Crathie Parish Church (1893–95) [157], the local church of 'royal Balmoral', the grey granite simplicity echoes the supposed Presbyterian beliefs of the monarchy when visiting Scotland. Important examples by other designers include Burnet's Gardner Memorial Church in Brechin, Angus (1896–1900), and a succession of scholarly neo-Romanesque churches stretching into the early 20th century by Peter MacGregor Chalmers (1859–1922), e.g. St Leonard's, Dunfermline (1903), Kirn (1906–7), and St Nicholas's, Prestwick (1908).

The Cult of the House

These attempts to re-assert monumental dignity, as a cure for the excesses of stylistic historicism, were hardly novel. More innovative and polemical were the moves to build on the English Arts and Crafts critique of industrial modernity and adopt a free, artistic approach inspired by pre-industrial life. Art was to provide an escape from the masks of public culture. The focus of this polemical movement was the home. Already, the suburban house was established as a redoubt for the rich against the excesses and lack of privacy of the city. Now, with the growth of the mass nation-state, the collective ethical force once attributed to institutions such as museums and parliaments was transferred to the ordinary home. This was the place where the wounds of modern society could be healed, and national identity could best be fostered.

In such a context, the old type of ornament-encrusted villa became as objectionable as any other commercialized building type – or so argued the advocates of 'artistic' or 'aesthetic' interiors and 'homely' exteriors, opponents of mass industrial decoration who flourished in England in the wake of the Gothic Revival. Renouncing the longstanding Glasgow tradition of interior decoration using industrial techniques, Scottish architects were prominent in this Domestic Revival movement. Norman Shaw had pioneered the informal half-timbered 'Old English' style in the Sussex countryside, at Glen Andred (1867) and Leyswood (1868–69). Shortly afterwards, J. J. Stevenson (1831–1908), a friend of Alexander Thomson and one of the pioneers of the SPAB (Society for the Protection of Ancient Buildings), designed one of the first examples of the 'Queen Anne style' of artisan mannerist

brick town-houses, the Red House in Kensington, London (1871). The naturalization of the Domestic Revival in Scotland, under the label of 'Traditionalism', was the work of Rowand Anderson. In his own Edinburgh suburban villa, Allermuir (1879–82) [158], he devised a Scottish rubble-built equivalent of Queen Anne, inspired by 17th-century 'homely' classicism, with an informal interior stocked with antique furniture and china. At the same time, Anderson began work on the definitive artistic retreat: an escapist palace at Mount Stuart on the Isle of Bute, for John Patrick, 3rd Marquess of Bute. The Marquess, a prodigiously wealthy landowner who had opted for a life of romantic Catholic medievalism, commissioned Anderson in 1878 to rebuild the fire-damaged Mount Stuart as a refined Gothic palazzo [159]. The house is crammed with astrological and mystical decoration, with a grand columned stair, a lantern-crowned chapel (added in 1897–1902), and a vast marble- and alabaster-lined hall at the centre; a formidable apparatus of domestic technology, including a pioneering electric lighting installation, was carefully hidden behind the scenes.

After 1880, a wide range of Scottish architects embraced the ideal of the 'artistic' escapist home, and integrated it with the existing Scotch Baronial style. In the houses and villas of William Leiper from the 1870s (e.g. Kinlochmoidart, Lochaber, 1883), the result was an effective synthesis of simplified Baronial exterior and refined 'aesthetic' interior. At the other extreme, some English or English-based architects grafted Scottish features on to Arts and Crafts cottages or houses: James M. Maclaren (1843–90) built a group of thatched farm buildings in Glenlyon, Perthshire, in 1889–91, while W. R. Lethaby (1857–1931) designed a hybrid Scoto-Cotswold manor-house and chapel at Melsetter, Orkney, in 1898.

The most effective Traditionalist homes were not new buildings at all, but old houses or castles that had been restored, in the restrained manner advocated by William Morris. The modern conservation movement in Scotland began not with cathedrals and churches but as an integral part of the 'cult of the house'. At Earlshall, Fife [160], the young Robert Lorimer (1864–1929), an Anderson pupil who would become Edinburgh's leading architect in the 1920s, meticulously restored a small castle and formal walled garden in 1890–94, evoking (in his own words) the 'dignified and yet liveable' restraint of 'a Scotch gentleman's home'.

At the end of this 'golden century' of Scottish architecture, then, the ideal of the home was still a relatively élitist affair; but

158 Allermuir, Colinton, Edinburgh, by R. Rowand Anderson, 1879–82. This photograph, taken c. 1900, shows Anderson putting in his garden.

159 Mount Stuart, Bute, by R. Rowand Anderson. The original square block, designed by Anderson in 1879–80 and built in 1880–85, draws on the late medieval secular architecture of France and Italy, and contains a vast marbled central hall, staircase and gallery – interiors which took some twenty years to finish. The right-hand tower was truncated in the mid-1890s after a storm. The chapel (partly visible far left) was added in 1897–1902.

160 Earlshall, Fife, restoration and landscaping scheme by R. S. Lorimer, 1890–94. The original castle, a late 16th-century courtyard complex of house and offices, is roughly comparable in date and character to Edzell (ill. 55). Lorimer created a large walled garden wrapped round three sides, complete with geometrical flower beds and pavilions. The doocot in the field on the left is probably of c. 1600. This exhibition drawing was prepared by John Begg, who subsequently became a prominent Edinburgh Traditionalist architect.

that was already changing. The move towards more dispersed, domestic layouts in institutions such as lunatic asylums or the Bridge of Weir Orphan Colony near Glasgow, built from 1876 by philanthropist William Quarrier, signalled a desire to extend the healing, soothing qualities of the architect-designed home to more disadvantaged groups in society. The growing tension between individualist and collective visions was summed up in one dramatic juxtaposition on the northern edge of Edinburgh's New Town. Here, in 1883, the newspaper publisher J. R. Findlay commissioned Sydney Mitchell to design two sharply contrasting projects: a sumptuous townhouse for himself in Rothesay Terrace, in a subtly modified 'aesthetic' variant of late New Town classicism; and Well

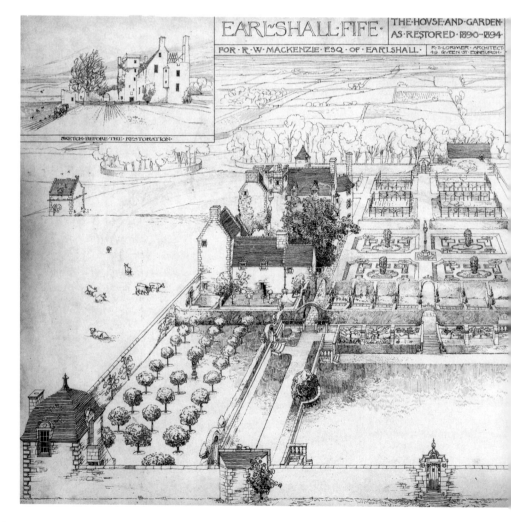

EARLSHALL·FIFE· THE·HOVSE·AND·GARDEN·
AS·RESTORED·1890–1894·
FOR·R·W·MACKENZIE·ESQ·OF·EARLSHALL· R·S·LORIMER·ARCHITECT
49·QVEEN·ST·EDINBVRGH·

SKETCH·BEFORE·THE·RESTORATION·

161 Well Court, Edinburgh, by A. G. Sydney Mitchell, begun in 1883, seen across the Water of Leith from J. R. Findlay's townhouse high above in Rothesay Terrace.

Court, a steep-roofed, Arts and Crafts Old Town-style courtyard block, containing tenements for his newspaper workforce, and situated just across a dramatic gorge from his own house. From Findlay's drawing room, he could view his philanthropic project from above, as a picturesque landscape object, like an old German walled city in a painting [161]. All this was still rooted in Victorian paternalism. But in the coming 20th century, the ideal of 'community planning' would be freed from the complex hierarchies of class, and extended across the entire country.

Chapter 6   The 20th Century: Building the Social Nation

For much of the 20th century, Scottish architecture was dominated by a violent reaction against the Victorian age: there was, for several decades, an almost complete shift towards a collective modern world of disciplined mass movements. This was a chastening time, like an extended hangover after a lavish party. Despite an overall increase in general living standards, a nagging perception of relative decline robbed new Scottish architecture of much of its potential shine. At the same time, strenuous efforts were made to expunge the now embarrassing legacy of the 'golden century', beginning in the 1920s with the demolition of Hamilton Palace, and proceeding in the 1950s to a surgical assault on the fabric of the industrial cities.

Two Pioneers: Mackintosh and Geddes
The Modernist world-view took several decades to emerge from its predecessor, and its two most influential Scottish participants – Charles Rennie Mackintosh (1868–1928) and Patrick Geddes (1854–1932) – came at the beginning of the process, when the bold individualism of the late 19th century was still dominant.
    Mackintosh's work continued the Aesthetic Movement revolt from public monumentality towards the subjective refuge of the home, doing this now through a highly charged and all-embracing artistic vision. In declamatory language reminiscent of his allies, the Austrian and German 'Secessionists' (a branch of the international Art Nouveau), he proclaimed in 1902 that his 'modern individual art', with its 'hallucinating character', was 'like an escape into the mountain air from the stagnant vapours of a morass'. He rejected historicism and façade ornament for a novel, personal style. This was composed of natural, symbolist and geometrical elements, initially emphasizing sinuous or curved

162 Floodlit night view of the 1938 Glasgow Empire Exhibition, including two of the chief Art Deco setpieces: in the foreground, the Imperial Chemical Industries pavilion (by Basil Spence) with its ring of three pylons and Thomas Whalen sculptures; behind to the right, the stepped, silver-painted Tower of Empire (by Thomas S. Tait, with Launcelot Ross and the engineer Thomas Mearns), with its balconies and bright blue fin.

163 Glasgow School of Art,
by C. R. Mackintosh (Honeyman
& Keppie), from 1896: main façade.
The large windows light studios;
the window to the left of the
entrance door lights the janitor's
office; the director's office (lit by
the large arched window) is above,
with its own small studio on the
second floor.

164 St Andrew's East Church
Glasgow, by James Miller, 1903–4:
the towered, arched façade.

forms and 'Celtic mysticism'. Mackintosh's key works, designed under the aegis of his partnership with John Honeyman (1831–1914) and John Keppie (1863–1945), spanned the mid- to late 1890s and early 1900s. They included a number of interior schemes for houses and tearooms; several complete villas, the most important being Hill House, in the Clyde resort of Helensburgh [166]; and a small number of public, religious and commercial buildings, including his chief work, Glasgow School of Art [163, 171, 172]; there was also a remarkable design of 1901 for a 'Haus eines Kunstfreundes' (Art Lover's House), drawn up as part of a competition sponsored by a German interior design magazine [167].

In general, there was a sharp dichotomy between Mackintosh's designs for exteriors and interiors. The exteriors were essentially a late, geometrical version of Scotch Baronial, offset by accentuated touches of individualism to distinguish them from conventional monumental Scottish public architecture. Here, Mackintosh looked for inspiration to the work of English Arts and Crafts designers such as C. R. Lethaby or C. F. A. Voysey (1857–1941). His first works for Honeyman & Keppie retained elements of classical regularity, offset by Arts and Crafts or Art Nouveau gestures – for instance, the sinuously modelled corner tower of the Glasgow Herald Building (1893–94). Some later urban designs continued to combine a general regularity with more personal elements, as at the twin-towered Scotland Street School, Glasgow (1902–6) or the tightly confined, Daily Record Building, Glasgow (1900), which exploited its narrow site with soaring bay windows. In the original block of the Glasgow School of Art (1896–99), the steeply sloping site was exploited with Baronial panache, with dramatic projecting wings at the side and rear, including a tall rubble east façade dotted with small irregular openings. On the north-facing main façade [163], Mackintosh offset the regularity of the main row of large studio windows by quirkish asymmetrical elements and details, including an arched entrance portal of an asymmetrical Arts and Crafts kind. In his Queen's Cross Church, Glasgow (1897), Mackintosh combined Art Nouveau details with an Arts and Crafts Perpendicular Gothic – as did the prolific James Miller (1860–1947), somewhat more spectacularly, at St Andrew's East Church, Glasgow (1903–4) [164], with its twin towers and linking arch that recall Fyvie Castle [60]. Mackintosh's domestic work (like that of his Secession friends) set out to evoke the severe geometry of the pre-industrial age, but combined cottage-like modesty with elements of Baronial

rhetoric, in houses such as Windyhill at Kilmacolm, Renfrewshire (1899), and Hill House (1902–4) [166]. The 'Haus eines Kunstfreundes' was more symmetrical, like a 17th-century laird's house.

In Mackintosh's interiors, the traditional stylistic contrasts between rooms, especially between dark 'masculine' and light 'feminine' spaces, were transformed into a more abstract and reposeful spatial and formal patterning, including carefully placed furniture and fittings, and intense areas of decoration, designed by the architect and his wife, Margaret Macdonald (1865–1933). The most significant series of interiors began in the later 1890s, with their increasingly dominant contributions to a series of tea rooms in Glasgow for Kate Cranston: Buchanan Street (1896), Argyle Street (1897) and Ingram Street (1901). The climax of the series was the Willow Tea Rooms (1903), whose abstractly harled, Secession-style façade [165] gave access to a flowing sequence of dark and light spaces, culminating in the intense, glittering Salon de Luxe, with a stained glass door and large gesso panel by Macdonald. Mackintosh and Macdonald's main domestic interiors date from 1899 onwards, including their own flat at 120 Mains Street, Glasgow, and the interiors of Windyhill and Hill House. The spatial play between sombre and brilliantly light rooms reached its climax in the 'Haus eines Kunstfreundes' design, with a dining room ringed with gridded, dark-stained wall panels, and a music room [167] in airy light grey, offset by splashes of vivid colour and a piano with baldacchino.

Although Patrick Geddes was not an architect but a biologist and city planner, his work also stressed the way in which art could enhance the psychic health of individuals and communities. As a supporter of scientific evolution, Geddes aspired to advance from a lower to a higher ('Neotechnic') culture, grounded in both rational and spiritual values as against what he saw as the barbarity of laissez-faire capitalism. He aimed to foster a renewal of urban culture, using the Edinburgh Old Town as a laboratory of 'renascence'. Geddes's developments were grounded in a wider social and geographical analysis of the city in its regional context, which was to be achieved through a procedure of survey and planning. Architecturally, regeneration was to be brought about by a process of 'conservative surgery', by which Geddes meant small-scale, organic interventions to bring greenery, space and artistic architecture to the slums: his concern was, however, not with socialist egalitarianism but with what he saw as cultural renewal. From the 1890s, he began to apply this formula to the Old Town,

165 Willow Tea Rooms, Glasgow, by C. R. Mackintosh (Honeyman, Keppie & Mackintosh), 1903: the façade seen in its original condition.

166 Hill House, Helensburgh, by C. R. Mackintosh (Honeyman, Keppie & Mackintosh), 1902–4, photographed when newly completed.

167 C. R. Mackintosh: competition design for a 'Haus eines Kunstfreundes' (Art Lover's House), 1901: the music room. (From *Meister der Innenkunst: Charles Rennie Mackintosh, Glasgow: Haus eines Kunstfreundes*, published by A. Koch, Darmstadt, 1902)

168 Ramsay Garden, Edinburgh, by A. G. Sydney Mitchell and S. Henbest Capper (with Patrick Geddes), 1892–94. This picturesquely massed reconstruction and enlargement of a group of 18th-century buildings imported the 'Old Edinburgh' style of Well Court (ill. 161) into the heart of the Old Town itself.

in a series of dense, picturesque projects which developed the ideas of Mitchell's Well Court [161]. The largest and most important was Ramsay Garden (1892–94) [168], partly designed by Mitchell himself, along with S. Henbest Capper (1860–1924): a vertiginous, turreted and gabled cluster of apartments for intellectuals, situated right beside Edinburgh Castle.

Both Mackintosh and Geddes were giants of the modern age; but in the short term their subjective, individualistic approach appeared more like an anachronistic aberration. Although Geddes's fusion of idealism and pragmatism would influence generations of Modernist planners, he himself only produced one major city plan – that for Tel Aviv-Yafo in Palestine (1925), in the form of a grid of 'super-blocks' containing collective open spaces, doubtless inspired by the Edinburgh New Town. The only immediate outcome of Geddes' philosophy at home would be the growth of an indigenous Scottish conservation movement, fostered in the 1930s by the 4th Marquess of Bute through the restoration work of the architect Robert Hurd (1905–63) and the pioneering Old Town inventories of Ian Lindsay (1906–66).

The Return to Order

By 1905, Scottish architecture had been overtaken by a very different type of modernity – a disciplined 'return to order', which would predominate for much of the 20th century. This consolidated the revival of traditional order that had begun in 1880–1900, and was focused on the grand public and imperial building programmes of the turn of the century. After Britain's political rapprochement with France in 1904, it took on a new form: the cry went up for a monumental Beaux-Arts architecture and city planning, to replace English Baroque individualism. Burnet was the natural leader of this new fashion, and he was invited down to London to design the most prestigious public building of the decade, a great extension to the British Museum (1905–14) [169].

169 King Edward VII Galleries, British Museum, London, by J. J. Burnet, 1905–14.

He fronted this with a restrained giant colonnade, typically
neoclassical in its under-emphasized centre: the entire front is
subtly battered, in line with the outer framing pylons [169]. From
that point, the planning of public buildings and civic centres across
Britain was shaped by this stately dignity, not least in Scotland
itself. Even a utilitarian institution such as Glasgow's giant new
Royal Technical College (1902–11) could take on a sublime
Beaux-Arts grandeur, in its arched and buttressed design by
David Barclay.

These changes were supported by developments in building
technology, especially the popularization of steel-framing from
around 1905, which encouraged a more simplified and cubic

approach to commercial architecture. In the Kodak office in Kingsway, London (1910), or the Wallace Scott factory, Glasgow (1913), Burnet abandoned his heavily modelled classical manner, stripping the heavy walling from the frame and the windows: Wallace Scott, with its corner pylons and repetitive windows, was like a simplified version of the British Museum colonnade. Another response was to treat the walling as a shallowly modelled skin. Examples include the rippling, bay-windowed façade of the Northern Insurance building in Glasgow of 1908–9 by John A. Campbell (1859–1909) [170] and a remarkable series of London office blocks designed by J. J. Joass (1868–1952) in partnership with John Belcher (1841–1913), featuring a restless, explicitly Mannerist vertical incrustation of windows and walling features. Mackintosh's last major works, from around 1905 onwards, echoed these developments at one remove, adopting a more geometrical, gridded manner of subdividing space in the new interiors of 1910–11 at the Ingram Street Tea Rooms, and anticipating the complexities of Cubism in his interior work

171 Glasgow School of Art west wing, by C. R. Mackintosh (Honeyman, Keppie & Mackintosh), 1905–9: interior of the library.

of 1916 at 78 Derngate, Northampton. The new west wing which completed the Glasgow School of Art (1905–9) was built in a more stylized, linear manner than the remainder, including a grand array of slender oriels on the steeply descending west façade [172]. These oriels lit the new library, whose central space was defined by a complex grid of galleries, projecting supports and hanging light-fittings, decorated with notched and geometrical patterns [171].

After the First World War, the modern Beaux-Arts movement increasingly turned to America as the symbolic home of Progress. The London branch of Burnet's practice became the leading representative in the British Empire of the practical but stylish modernity associated with large American firms. This 'Art Deco' approach was quite unlike the nervously energetic Continental avant-garde factions (Expressionism, De Stijl, etc.). It was versatile, boldly styled when necessary with the latest Modernist motifs, but oriented towards the client's requirements rather than any elevated utopian vision. Burnet's modernity developed organically out of 19th-century Glasgow eclecticism: his main post-war partner, Thomas S. Tait (1882–1954), had been apprenticed to Alexander Thomson's chief assistant.

At first, the main thrust of Burnet and Tait's work was a development of the firm's pre-war commercial architecture, in a succession of steel-framed office buildings and department stores. Increasingly, Tait emphasized an architecture of 'mass', of cubic blocks ranged in pyramidal, stepped forms, with punched-in rows of windows and columns, and exotic incised detail, all under the influence both of American skyscrapers and of Thomson's urban buildings. The pioneering post-war building in this style was Adelaide House, London (1920–25), a monumental, cubic office block by the Thames, with an 'Egyptian' battered profile, crowned by a pilastered attic. During the later 1920s, the growing economic crisis prompted Burnet and Tait to turn to more 'social' building types, and more varied types of Art Deco styling. Projects such as the Royal Masonic Hospital, London (1930–33), were dealt with by Tait in an unsentimental manner, often clad in a restrained Dutch brick Modernism. For monumental state buildings, a grandiose stone-clad heaviness was thought more appropriate. In 1937–39, when the time came to build a new administrative headquarters for newly devolved 'Scottish Office' government functions, St Andrew's House in Edinburgh [173], Tait designed an integrated, pyramidally massed and, in his words, 'sculpturesque' building, exploiting the dramatic site once occupied by Adam's

172 Glasgow School of Art west wing, by C. R. Mackintosh (Honeyman, Keppie & Mackintosh), 1905–9: detail of oriels on the west façade.

Bridewell on the flank of Calton Hill. Burnet and Tait's firm also helped give Art Deco styling to some of the world's most prominent infrastructure works, including the Sydney Harbour Bridge in Australia (1924–32) [174], where massively battered portal piers were designed to balance the vast curve of the trusses.

In the field of civic design, Tait's solutions were very different from Geddes' organic 'conservative surgery'. From 1926, at the instigation of the firm of Crittall, makers of metal-framed windows, Tait designed a pioneering company village of flat-roofed white houses at Silver End, Essex. In 1937–38, he applied a more uncompromising urban axiality to the planning of the influential Glasgow Empire Exhibition, the first of many symbolic attempts to reverse Glasgow's decline. The Exhibition was composed of orderly arrays of white, steel-framed, prefabricated pavilions, floodlit in bright colours at night. The site was crowned by the extravagantly Art Deco 'Tower of Empire', nearly 100 metres (some 300 feet) high [162].

It was a mark of the continuing convergence between western and eastern Scotland that the Anderson/Lorimer school of Traditionalists pursued a generally similar 'return to order'. For a time, their interest shifted firmly to monumental buildings. After 1900 Robert Lorimer had begun to build a new type of confidently

173 St Andrew's House, Edinburgh, by Thomas S. Tait (Burnet, Tait & Lorne), 1937–39, photographed when new. In the background are several Calton Hill monuments: from left to right, they are the porticoed City Observatory (W. H. Playfair, 1818), the Gaol Governor's House (Archibald Elliot, 1815–17), the Nelson Monument (Robert Burn, 1807), and, extreme right, the Royal High School (Thomas Hamilton, 1825–29: see ill. 112).

massed country house in exposed rubble; examples include Ardkinglas, Argyll (1905–7), and Formakin, Renfrewshire (1912–14). The Thistle Chapel that he added to St Giles's Cathedral in Edinburgh (1909–11) [175] took the 'renascence of worship' tendencies of the previous decades to a microcosmic extreme of intensity. After the War, all these religious and symbolic crafts elements coalesced in Lorimer's designs for the Scottish National War Memorial, adapted in 1924–27 from an old barracks block on the summit of the Edinburgh Castle rock [176]. The rubble-built shell was turned into a Hall of Honour in a massive Scots Renaissance style; entered by a tall, sombre portal and lit from stained-glass windows by Edinburgh crafts designers, it contained a profusion of memorials. Other east coast Traditionalist architects, notably Leslie Grahame Thomson (1896–1974) and Reginald Fairlie (1883–1952), followed Lorimer in using archaic rubble primitivism for some public buildings, including churches, and Arts and Crafts classicism for others. The early 20th-century work of the Aberdonian architect Ninian Comper (1864–1960) – for example St Mary's, Wellingborough, Northamptonshire (1904–31), and St John's, Rothiemurchus, Inverness-shire (1928–31) – branched out in a different direction from the same Arts and Crafts stem, towards a synthesis of classical, Byzantine and Gothic church architecture (what Comper called 'unity by inclusion').

The culmination of the monumental public building phase of Traditionalism came after World War II, in the programme of

175 Thistle Chapel, St Giles's Cathedral, Edinburgh, by R. S. Lorimer, 1909–11.

176 Scottish National War Memorial, Edinburgh Castle, by Lorimer & Matthew, 1924–27 (see also ill. 46). An old barracks block was gutted, given a new façade, and extended at the rear by the addition of the 'Shrine', an exaggeratedly tall medievalizing apse perched on exposed rock, which contained a steel casket with the names of all the Scottish war dead. This 1928 view shows the façade with wreaths laid in commemoration of the death of Earl Haig, wartime commander and head of the Royal British Legion.

classical power stations and concrete dams commissioned in the late 1940s and early 1950s from architects such as James Shearer (1881–1962) by the newly founded North of Scotland Hydro-Electric Board, in often wild and sublime settings across the Highlands. Perhaps the most notable example was Shearer and (George) Annand's Fasnakyle, Inverness-shire (1946–52), an asymmetrical, cubic, rubble-built group featuring sculptural panels of 'Celtic legends' by Hew Lorimer (1907–73), the sculptor son of Robert Lorimer.

The Modern Movement and Clydeside Reconstruction
But by the time the Hydro Board power stations were being built a new climate of architecture, more openly responsive to the mass society of the 20th century, had emerged. The governing agenda was still the same as that of Improvement, namely material betterment harnessed to secular utopian ideals. But the preferred means had changed from the individual to the collective, especially in the warlike climate of the 1940s and early 1950s. The overriding aim was the building of 'community', which was seen at first as something new, hygienic and rational. In response, the Functionalist strand within Modernism emphasized large-scale, standardized building on scientifically defined lines, and took as its symbol the tower block set in open space and greenery, breaking from the old horizontal, dense city of façades and mixed-together uses. The collectivist principles of Modernism involved a partial flattening out of the old hierarchy of architecture. No longer were important buildings to be marked out by the addition of historicist ornament: instead, 'higher' architectural value was integrated with the building itself. Yet there was still a demand for symbolism, monumentality, even 'image' in architecture.

The focus of the new concern with state-led planning was the urban west of Scotland. Here the old confident global outlook had vanished, and the built environment created by the Victorians was now seen as a disgrace – a 'Glasgow problem' of congestion, slums and obsolescence, which was to be put right by the apparatus of disciplined state power. But whereas in the 19th century the dynamism of Glasgow's culture had stimulated the most diverse architecture of Victorian Scotland, now the city's reconstruction activity was dominated by vigorous but utilitarian municipal production leaders. The Housing Committee Convener David Gibson was an impassioned 'housing crusader' who grasped at the Modernist tower block as a way of circumventing land shortages and maintaining production. Gibson's boldest projects were Red

177 Sighthill council housing development, Glasgow, by Crudens Ltd (with Glasgow Corporation Department of Architecture and Planning), 1963–69: a grandiose 'package-deal' project of ten 20-storey blocks (arranged in Functionalist parallel lines, or *Zeilenbau*), low-rise flats, and primary schools, sited on a reclaimed chemical wasteground.

Road of 1962–69, designed by Sam Bunton, an outcrop of sheer 31-storey towers and slabs, and Sighthill of 1963–69 [177], with ten 20-storey slabs, designed by the building contractors Crudens. Here the two essential elements of Modernist urbanism – artistic life and utopian idealism – were both stripped away, leaving only a gargantuan, almost pre-Modernist monumentality.

This militant utilitarianism provoked the emergence of an equally uncompromising art-for-art's-sake faction in Glasgow, in the individualistic architecture of Gillespie, Kidd & Coia. Inspired ultimately by the poetic élitism of Mackintosh, they built a succession of churches and public buildings, mainly for the Catholic Church, while avoiding the more contentious social building types, such as tower blocks. From the 1930s to the late 1950s, the practice was dominated by Jack Coia (1898–1981), who designed roomy brick churches with Italian Baroque overtones. From the mid-1950s, two younger partners, Isi Metzstein (b. 1928) and Andrew MacMillan (b. 1928), launched into a more assertively sculptural approach, inspired by the later style of Le Corbusier. They pioneered a new pattern of single-volume, dramatically toplit churches, beginning with St Paul's, Glenrothes, Fife (1956–57), and culminating in the Albi-like brick outcrop of St Bride's, East Kilbride (1964), and the soaring, prow-like St Benedict's, Drumchapel, Glasgow (1965–67). At the same time, they devised an ingenious, agglomerative pattern for large educational and residential buildings, including a complex seminary extension at

Cardross near Dumbarton, St Peter's College (1959–66) [178], with stepped accommodation blocks and jutting concrete chapels rising from wooded landscape. The experience of these extravagantly poetic buildings by users was marred by a series of structural and maintenance problems, culminating in the demolition of some churches and the abandonment of Cardross Seminary after only fourteen years of active use.

This debilitating polarization between artistic and engineering solutions left post-war Clydeside architecture wide open to external intervention. The most ambitious challenge came from the burgeoning movement of modern regional planning. This combined Geddes' idea of place-sensitive survey and plan, the theory of planned new towns proposed by Ebenezer Howard (notably in *Garden Cities of To-Morrow*, 1902), and the Modernist love of flowing space and greenery. In 1946, a decentralization strategy of green belts and new towns was put forward by Patrick Abercrombie and Robert Matthew in their Clyde Valley Regional Plan; the first new town to be commenced in Scotland, East Kilbride (from 1947), was a relatively orthodox example of sprawling 1940s 'neighbourhood unit' planning, laid out by Scottish Office architect-planners, with the first low-rise areas (e.g. in The Murray) completed around 1952. By contrast, the second of the Clydeside new towns, Cumbernauld [179], founded in 1956 and planned in outline from 1958, drew on the most avant-garde strands of British planning thought. While retaining the Modernist insistence on new community building and technocratic

178 St Peter's College, Cardross, by Gillespie, Kidd & Coia, 1959–66. This seminary project was the culmination of the practice's long series of religious and educational projects for the West of Scotland Catholic community. Here we see the main entrance to the accommodation block, massively built using in-situ concrete construction, with the tiered accommodation floors stepping backwards above the continuous window-band of the communal areas and chapel.

179 Cumbernauld New Town: aerial view in 1967. In the foreground is the almost-completed Town Centre Phase 1, by Geoffrey Copcutt/Cumbernauld New Town Development Corporation, of 1963–67; in the background, the 'Bison' point blocks and terraces of the Seafar and Ravenswood areas, built from 1961 by Cumbernauld New Town Development Corporation architects and, in the case of the point blocks, the architects of Concrete Scotland Ltd.

direction, Cumbernauld emphasized the need for a more dense urban texture through a tighter clustering of the housing zone, and the inclusion of a multi-function, multi-level ('megastructural') town centre, planned from 1959 and built in 1963–67, for which the project architect was Geoffrey Copcutt. Cumbernauld's dynamic planning concept made a decisive contribution to the international debate about urban density and zoning, and the town as built became a magnet for overseas visitors. In 1967 the American Institute of Architects, awarding Cumbernauld a prestigious prize for 'community architecture', declared that it was 'designed for the millennium – the dreams of the 1920s and 1930s are being built on a hill near Glasgow'.

Robert Matthew and Basil Spence: Two Modernisms

Most of the Cumbernauld architects and planners were English, but the fragmentation of Glasgow post-war architecture also left the field open to Edinburgh, whose two chief figures, Robert Matthew (1906–75) and Basil Spence (1907–76), inherited the Burnet mantle of strong London and international links. Matthew and Spence had studied at the same time at Edinburgh College of Art, where they had once formed the two halves of a pantomime horse in a college play. Now, separately, they seemed to bestride Modern architecture in Scotland (and were knighted in 1962 and

1960 respectively). This dominance was illustrated by the fact that when, in 1957, Glasgow Corporation's architectural department embarked on a highly publicized redevelopment of the notorious Gorbals slum area, just south-east of the city centre, they went straight to Matthew and Spence, who were commissioned in 1958 to design separate, although adjacent, multi-storey projects [180].

The differing approaches of Matthew and Spence acted as legitimizing forces for the varied strands of Modernism in Scotland. Of the two, it was arguably Matthew who engaged with the ideals of the Modern Movement in a more direct manner. His father, John F. Matthew (1875–1955), had been the partner of Robert Lorimer, and Robert had grown up steeped in Edinburgh Traditionalism and the ideas of Geddes. But from the early 1930s, he committed himself instead to Modernism and the ideal of the public architect. In 1943–46, Matthew organized the setting up of a government regional planning service for Scotland. Then, at the age of only thirty-nine, he secured the premier post in public architecture in Britain, that of Architect to the London County Council. At the LCC he played a key role in the conception and

180 Hutchesontown/Gorbals redevelopment area, Glasgow, 'cleared' and rebuilt with council housing between 1956 and 1974: aerial view in 1965. At the centre are the somewhat conservative four-storey maisonette blocks of Area A by the Corporation planners, 1956–58. At top left are the 18-storey towers and low blocks of Area B by Robert Matthew and Johnson-Marshall, 1958–64. At the lower right are the two monumental 20-storey slab blocks of Area C by Basil Spence, 1958–66 (demolished 1993). Spence fancifully speculated in 1958 that the great indented collective balconies of his blocks could be used for clothes drying, creating the image of a 'great ship in full sail' on wash-day.

design of the Royal Festival Hall (1948–51) as a Geddes-like 'cultural centre', personally devising its innovative plan-form, with the auditorium insulated by foyers on all sides; and he ensured that the LCC Housing Division became a nursery of innovative welfare-state urbanism in England, nurturing a variety of competing factions of young architects dedicated to social building, and popularizing the tower block and other Modernist design forms.

In 1953 Matthew returned home to Edinburgh, and set up his own private practice and university department, which acted as an incubator of modern design in Scotland. On a visit to Scandinavia he had been shocked to discover that key architects such as Ragnar Østberg and Alvar Aalto had never even heard of Lorimer, despite the latter's reputation in Scotland. Matthew became convinced that the International Modern Movement was the only way forward for Scottish architecture. Indeed, his post-1953 practice and university department nurtured an entire generation of younger Modernist designers. But in some of his own early Scottish designs, such as Turnhouse Airport near Edinburgh (1953–56) [181], Crombie Hall, Aberdeen University (1954–58), Queen's College Tower, Dundee (1955–61) [182], and power stations in the Breadalbane project, Perthshire (1956–60), he followed a Geddesian strategy of rooting the new architecture in 'vernacular' materials and traditions, including rubble and timber cladding.

181 Turnhouse Airport, near Edinburgh, by Robert Matthew, 1953–56: perspective by Matthew's assistant (later partner) Tom Spaven, 1953. This modestly scaled building, the first commission of Matthew's post-1953 private practice, inaugurated his 'vernacular' phase, in its combination of timber and rubble cladding with modern steel-framed construction.

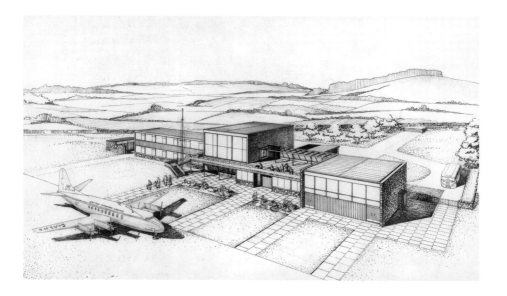

182 Tower Building, Queen's College, Dundee, by Robert Matthew and Johnson-Marshall, 1955–61: a bold and idiosyncratic extension of the 'vernacular' picturesque, complete with full-height rubble cladding, to the scale of a 12-storey tower block. The jutting-out section on the fourth floor expresses the Senate Room. A new three-storey university library stretches from the other side of the tower.

In 1956 Matthew joined with the English schools specialist Stirrat Johnson-Marshall (1912–81) to form the firm of Robert Matthew and Johnson-Marshall. RMJM tackled the full range of welfare-state building and planning projects across the United Kingdom, as well as development work throughout the Commonwealth. Its work pointed away from the strict ideal of the public architect towards a private, multi-disciplinary firm of designers and planners. Matthew's own specific design contribution was confined to a minority of projects, among them New Zealand House (1955–63), an embassy complex which included, controversially, the first Modernist tower block in central London, and the Arts Faculty at Edinburgh University (1960–67), which similarly introduced the first high tower (the David Hume Tower) to central Edinburgh, demolishing part of the classical George Square in the process. Increasingly, younger RMJM partners took the design initiative. For instance, in the mid-1960s, John Richards (b. 1931) developed a sober style of emphatic horizontal elements,

183 Stirling University, by Robert Matthew, Johnson-Marshall & Partners: aerial view of the completed complex set in the landscaped Airthrey Castle estate, 1974. At top centre is the prefabricated, multi-purpose, single-storey Phase I (Pathfoot Building, 1966–67). At the left is the main permanent teaching and social area (Cottrell Building, 1969–70; Library and MacRobert Arts Centre, 1969–72). At the upper right are the halls of residence (1969–72).

seen in his project for Stirling University, whose prefabricated first stage (1966–67) was set in country-house parkland [183], and in the Royal Commonwealth Pool in Edinburgh (1965–70).

During the 1960s Matthew's own activity, like Burnet's before him, became focused on the wider field of planning consultancy and architectural diplomacy. For example, he became heavily involved in an attempt to introduce a modern planned economy to the devolved statelet of Northern Ireland; he drew up an Ulster equivalent of the Clyde Valley Plan in 1960–63, and a detailed design for the New University of Ulster at Coleraine (built 1968–77). Matthew flung himself like no previous – or subsequent – Scottish architect into the task of building international links and fostering friendships across the sharp divides of the mid-century. His proudest achievement was the foundation in 1965 of the Commonwealth Association of Architects, with its forthright policy of decolonization. And in 1963, as president of the Union Internationale des Architectes, he mediated in a confrontation over a UIA conference in Cuba, a role which obliged him one week to preside over a Communist-inspired competition for a monument to the Bay of Pigs invasion, and the next to chair a U.S.-inspired 'opposition' conference in Mexico!

The work of Basil Spence, by contrast with that of Matthew, still to some extent belonged to the pre-Modernist architectural world, with its hierarchy of status and rhetorical grandeur. Apprenticed initially to Sir Edwin Lutyens, Spence was a superlative draughtsman and artist, who in the later 1930s had worked in partnership with William Kininmonth (1904–88) on a highly eclectic range of buildings, including a new tower-house at Broughton, Peeblesshire (1935). After that, however, it was the Modern style that Spence applied to the design of a vast range of building types. Spence addressed head-on the challenge posed by postwar society to its architects: to renounce historical styles and ornament, while retaining the potential for symbolic monumentality. As a result, he was *the* architect of choice for the grandest state commissions – the buildings which were most closely bound up with the projection of British national identity. He built up his architecture of national symbolism on the foundation of extensive work in exhibition design, including the Sea and Ships building for the 1951 Festival of Britain in London, dramatically cut-away and sculpted beneath an overall metal framework [184]. In 1951, too, he secured the opportunity to apply those skills to the design of a great national building, when he won the competition for the new Coventry Cathedral, to replace the old cathedral gutted by bombing in 1940 [185]. His governing concept, inspired doubtless by the Scottish National War Memorial [176], was that the new cathedral should (in his own words) 'grow from the old', and he laid out a sequence of contrasting spaces, passing from the roofless ruins through a great canopy and glass window into the airily columned new building, with rippling side walls filled with large repetitive windows alluding

184 Sea and Ships Pavilion, Festival of Britain, London, by Basil Spence, 1951.

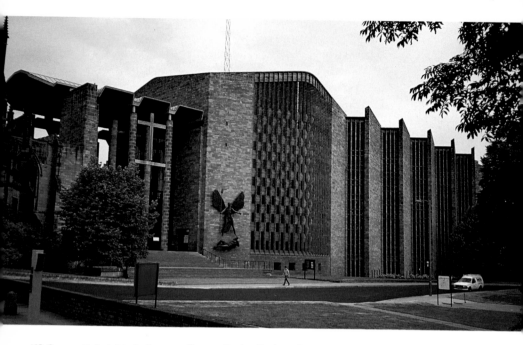

185 Coventry Cathedral, by Basil Spence, 1954–62. On the left is the lofty porch linking to the ruins of the old bombed cathedral; on the right, the sandstone-clad mass of the new building.

186 British Embassy Chancery, Rome, by Basil Spence, 1968–71. To circumvent local objections to development of the sensitive site, in gardens adjoining Michelangelo's Porta Pia, Spence designed the building as a low and relatively unobtrusive 'modern palazzo', travertine-clad and standing delicately on slender columns. The only really expansive gesture, a grand entrance staircase, was hidden away in the central courtyard.

187 British Pavilion, Expo 67, Montreal, Canada, by Basil Spence, 1965–67.

to Perpendicular Gothic. Coventry Cathedral was built in 1954–62, by which time Spence's international reputation had brought him a wealth of diverse commissions.

From 1951, Spence, like Burnet, ran separate Scottish and English practices. Within Britain, he designed for the full range of welfare-state activity while remaining faithful to his monumental design philosophy, emphasizing the honorific parts of a building in a manner reminiscent of contemporary architecture in the United States. He was most at home when tackling a symbolic government building, such as the British Embassy Chancery in Rome (built 1968–71), an office block which was treated as a grand pavilion in a formal landscaped garden, disguising its everyday function behind a modelled façade of travertine, standing on slender central columns. As consultant (from 1964) for an extension to the New Zealand Parliament House in Wellington, he conceived a massive, conical 11-storey block (dubbed the 'Beehive'), dwarfing the modest classical legislature of 1922. But it was still in exhibition design that Spence's 'modern monumentality' could be given the freest rein. In his British government pavilion (1965–67) for Expo 67 in Montreal [187], he adopted a very different approach to the lacy openness of the Sea and Ships Pavilion [184], designing a massive, windowless, jaggedly monumental outcrop – in his own words, 'a robust design in

which tradition and romance give way to a bold and uncompromising structure using large forms with an industrial bias . . . rough, simple, showing the mood of change in Britain'. Its tall tower, housing a 'Genius of Britain' display (designed by Beverley Pick), was crowned with Union Jack motifs and left open at the top, 'symbolising Britain's belief that her contributions to world progress are certainly far from finished'.

Even the building types of mass society, and the community ideals of utopianism, were 'monumentalized' in this way. In his section of the Gorbals redevelopment (1958–66) Spence adopted a radically different approach from Matthew's: with painterly romanticism, he designed two cliff-like, 20-storey slab blocks in ruggedly modelled concrete [180]. Spence's design for one of the English New Universities, Sussex University (built from 1960), was highly formal and monumental. Its first major building was a stately collegiate quadrangle block, Falmer House, dedicated solely to social and ceremonial functions, and dominated by a brick and concrete arch patterning inspired by Le Corbusier's Maisons Jaoul near Paris of 1951–55. Somewhat hybrid in character between social building and 'national monumentality' was his redevelopment of the Hyde Park cavalry barracks in London (built 1965–70) – one of the most grandly symbolic complexes of British military patriotism. Spence's solution ingeniously combined Modernist innovation and traditional imagery, by replanning the elongated site as an array of eight specialized blocks, separating out the stables, ceremonial entrance, and various categories of barracks and messes, including a tall, sculpturally crowned tower block housing the married quarters. His practice also maintained a large output of designs for commercial buildings, mostly of routinely Modernist character, but occasionally showing touches of his own personal flamboyance – for example in an abortive design of 1970, 'Project Z', for a prismatic skyscraper on a stepped podium, to house a mining conglomerate in Melbourne, Australia.

The work of Matthew and Spence set out a wide range of approaches to Modern design. Initially, it was Matthew's emphasis on the rationalistic, geometrical design of social architecture that made the widest impact in Scotland. As early as 1959, the architecture department of a large local authority, Lanark County Council, was able to design a vastly ambitious new headquarters for itself in the form of a curtain-walled 18-storey slab block, dominating the town of Hamilton. And the Scottish division of the National Coal Board, the department of Egon Riss, Chief

Production Architect, designed a succession of modern 'super-pits' in a starkly geometrical Functionalist form, with tall winding towers, including Killoch Colliery, Ayrshire (1953–60) [188], and Monktonhall Colliery, near Edinburgh (1965) – all now closed and demolished. The culmination of this 'scientific' strand of Scottish Modernism came much later, in the megastructure-like submersible platforms, redolent of the sci-fi utopianism of the Archigram Walking City concept, built in the 1970s for the North Sea oil industry. The Ninian Central platform, a concrete base 160 metres (525 feet) high supporting a complex steel superstructure, was hailed by its promoters as 'the biggest movable thing on earth' at the time of construction (1974–79).

More significant for the long run was a persistent strand of smaller-scale interventions in small-town or historic contexts, inspired by the Geddes formula of conservative surgery. Both Spence and Matthew gave early signals of allegiance to this approach, the former in a group of balconied, rubble-walled fishermen's houses in Dunbar, East Lothian (1949–52), and the latter in the Barshare development of 1957–62 at Cumnock, Ayrshire, designed on similar 'vernacular' lines. In the work of Wheeler & Sproson (chief partner Anthony Wheeler, b. 1919), based at Kirkcaldy in Fife, Geddesian conservative surgery

188 Killoch Colliery, Ochiltree, Ayrshire, by Egon Riss (National Coal Board, Scotland), 1953–60. This view shows the newly completed fan house and the No. 1 and 2 Shaft towers. Killoch was one of the NCB's Scottish 'super-pits' of the 1950s and 1960s. In 1965, it became the first Scottish colliery to produce one million tons of coal in a single year. It was closed in 1987, and demolished shortly afterwards.

was for the first time combined with a large-scale Modernist programme of social housing, in a variety of depressed historic towns in Fife and the Lothians. Some of these projects, such as Dysart, Fife (1958–71), were multi-phase redevelopments spanning many years, which avoided *tabula rasa* demolitions in favour of a complex tapestry of old and new. Other architects applied the same principles to the regeneration of historic towns up and down Scotland, such as Richard Moira (d. 1988), who worked with his wife, Betty (d. 1989), on a twenty-year housing programme in the Shetland capital of Lerwick [189].

By the late 1960s, this kind of collaboration of modernity and heritage gave way to a more confrontational relationship, fuelled by a growing public discontent with the scale and pace of Modernist redevelopments, and more generally by a growing crisis of confidence in the materialistic crusade of Progress, directed by experts. Robert Matthew made strenuous efforts to keep open the lines of communication, through a series of initiatives aimed at rehabilitating the decayed Edinburgh New Town, which culminated in 1970 in a grand international conference and the formation of the Edinburgh New Town Conservation Committee (1970). But by the late 1970s, the gulf had become unbridgeable, and the ever more militant conservation movement suddenly

189 The Lanes multi-phase redevelopment (council housing), Lerwick, Shetland, by Richard and Betty Moira, 1956–69: view of a newly completed infill phase in Mounthooly Street in 1965.

190 Burrell Collection Gallery, Glasgow, by Barry Gasson, John Meunier and Brit Andreson, 1971–83. The gallery's perimeter plan was focused on a courtyard and several reconstructed interiors from Hutton Castle, Berwickshire (the previous home of the collection). This view shows the gabled entrance, with the low and largely toplit main block behind. The woods of Pollok Park envelop the building on two sides.

found itself standing victorious over the collapsed remnants of the Modern Movement. The 1970s saw the lowest ebb of monumentality in new Scottish architecture. The most prestigious building project of the decade, the Burrell Collection [190], an art gallery sited in the woodland setting of Pollok Park in outer Glasgow, was won in a 1971 competition by three young Cambridge architects, Barry Gasson, John Meunier and Brit Andreson. Their design exploited the diversity of the collection through a complex 'perimeter plan', in which the main visitor route encircled a casbah-like warren of spaces. The exterior was self-effacing to an extreme, with one glazed façade appearing to dissolve in the adjacent woods.

From Postmodernism to Supermodernism

The last quarter of the 20th century was a time of ever more insistent demands for political self-rule, framed by the abortive conversion in 1977 of the Edinburgh Royal High School [112] into a parliament chamber and the construction from 1999 of a new parliament building at Holyrood [194]. But during this time Scottish architecture paradoxically underwent a marked decline in confidence and status. It was caught up, largely passively, in the growing movement of capitalist globalization, which rejected the Modern Movement's egalitarianism and high esteem of social building types. Architects were interested not in the regional synthesizing vision but in 'The City' as a theatre of 'mixed use' display or money-making. The new seats of moral authority were cultural-cum-capitalist complexes, such as museums and conference centres: it was accepted that each city or country must brand itself for the global market.

This new outlook involved the detachment of higher architectural value from the fabric of the building, and a renewed focus on façades, styles and the inspiration of the past. But there could be no question of reviving the old academic classical training, whose rules had provided a shortcut way to convey meaning in architecture. So the most relevant period of the past was inevitably the earlier 20th century, especially that strand which emphasized the individual creative genius, and which could now be turned into a signature architecture of competing, branded designers. The heritage that was exploited most relentlessly by Scottish Postmodernists was the work of Mackintosh. Its appeal lay in its multi-faceted character, reinforcing the artist-architect ideal with conservationism, civic pride, and kitsch commercialism. A range of Mackintosh motifs was popularized in Gillespie, Kidd & Coia's last major work, Robinson College in Cambridge (1974–80); in 1988, two years after the firm's dissolution, Andrew MacMillan was commissioned to construct a heritage centre in Glasgow based on the 'Haus eines Kunstfreundes' design. An earlier and more bizarre essay was the reconstruction within the brutalist Glasgow University Library and Museum complex by the English architect William Whitfield (dates?) of the interiors of a house where the Mackintoshes had lived; completed in 1982, this included a Victorian-style bay window – evoking that of the house – extruded from the flank of a tower block!

Postmodernist urbanism, in contrast to the vast horizons of Modernism, concentrated on bringing a mixed-use vitality to the inner city, through a combination of rehabilitation and jazzy new interventions. The special focus in Glasgow was the newly dubbed 'Merchant City', a neglected zone east of Buchanan Street. The firm of Elder & Cannon, for example, revitalized an entire street block, Ingram Square, in 1984–89, including new buildings in a light-hearted, colourful style akin to Art Deco.

When the demands for a home-rule parliament were finally met in May 1999 the inevitable architectural consequence was an upsurge in the rhetoric of 'Scottish pride'. But the expression of genuine cultural distinctiveness in architecture would now be a complicated task, as international architectural fashion had shifted from Postmodernism to a revived 'Modernist' style. Actually, the change from Postmodernism to 'Supermodernism' was largely skin-deep. The dominance of images, signature architects and market-driven building types grew stronger, and all that changed was the styling. This new approach, like that of Basil Spence, relied on grand gestures as a way of conveying elevated or symbolic content. In the simplest cases, this could be done with a context-free flamboyance, like a pavilion in a world's fair. Examples include the cluster of gleaming silvery shapes that make up the Glasgow Science Centre by BDP (Building Design Partnership) on the bank of the Clyde (1999–2001) and the giant tent-like structure designed by Michael Hopkins (b. 1935) for the Dynamic Earth theme park beside Edinburgh's Holyrood Park (1997–99). The continuing prestige of heritage dictated a balance between contextual respect and Supermodernist style. The latter no longer relied on the disciplined geometry of the 1950s but on more heterogeneous movements such as 'deconstruction', which abandoned any kind of unitary narratives. In some cases, the balance tilted heavily towards rhetorical show. For example, the Museum of Scotland in central Edinburgh of 1995–98 [191], by Benson & Forsyth (Gordon Benson and Alan Forsyth), although the extension of an existing museum building, was treated as an autonomous sculptural object, bursting out of its tightly confined site with busy Corbusian gestures and referential historical motifs, including a castle-like corner tower.

The conversion of old structures into multi-purpose arts centres was a particularly characteristic expression of this approach. The reconstruction of Mackintosh's Glasgow Herald

191 Museum of Scotland, Edinburgh, by Benson & Forsyth, 1995–98: perspective painting by Carl Laubin, 1994. (To the left of the new building is the round-arched façade of the original Royal Scottish Museum, by Captain Francis Fowke, 1860–61.) The new museum is entered through the circular corner tower. The main block behind contains a circulation courtyard surrounded by a complex warren of levels and cross-connections; the massive external walls are dotted with numerous small windows intended to frame historically significant views of the city. A rooftop terrace and restaurant serve the purpose of an 'outlook tower' over the historic city, echoing the ideas of Patrick Geddes.

Building as a new Glasgow architecture centre, the Lighthouse (1997–99), by Page & Park, involved the grafting of a dramatically vertical, glass-faced extension on to the side of the existing block, its design reverently related to the adjacent work of the 'master'. The younger Glasgow firm of Zoo Architects adopted a more raw, confrontational approach in the refurbishment of Glasgow's Tramway Theatre in 1998–2000, juxtaposing the rough brick shell of an old tram depot with the modernity of their steel and timber interventions. A related philosophy, more directly descended from Geddesian conservative surgery and previously pioneered in an influential series of private house extensions, was pursued by the Edinburgh architect Richard Murphy in his conversion of older structures into arts centres in Dundee (1998–99) and Stirling (1999–2001). The existing historic structure was treated as a masonry 'shell' or 'ruin' within which Murphy formed his characteristic intricate interlocking Supermodernist spaces and gestural, jutting roofline extrusions.

Another result of the accession of the first home-rule Scottish government in 1999 was a revival of emphasis on social building programmes, as part of a social-inclusion strategy designed to offset the ravages of market capitalism. Even here, however, the new stylistic individualism remained significant. For example, a new visitor centre at Edinburgh's Saughton Prison (1999), by the Glasgow architect Gareth Hoskins, evoked the formalist architecture of Gillespie, Kidd & Coia with its triangular copper-clad roof, white walling and irregularly windowed main frontage. In the Homes for the Future demonstration housing project overlooking Glasgow Green (from 1998), the unifying theme of white walling was offset by the diversity of designs by Elder & Cannon, Ushida Findlay, RMJM and others. In 2002, the Japanese/Scottish practice of Ushida Findlay extended their boldly

192 Museum of Scottish Country Life, East Kilbride, by Page & Park, 1998–2001. This new exhibition building, conceived in Geddesian terms as an 'outlook tower over rural Scotland', harked back in some ways to the 'vernacular' trends of postwar Scottish Modernism (e.g. the 1950s work of Robert Matthew or Alan Reiach). The building is constructed of precast concrete columns and slabs (externally rendered or timber-clad). Its plan is based on standardized grid dimensions, in order to express the museum's central principle of 'loose-fit' flexible storage – in striking contrast to the elaborately tailor-made spaces and forms of the Museum of Scotland (ill. 191).

193 Grafton New Hall, near Malpas, Cheshire, by Ushida Findlay: computer-generated perspective, 2002. The unobtrusive two-storey house, intended to look like a 'low sandstone outcrop . . . a geological remnant from the past or something eroded over time', comprises four sandstone-clad fingers, segregated by function in traditional country house style. These consist of family, visitor and leisure wings, and a culture wing with art gallery and cinema.

organic philosophy of housing design into a rural context in their project for Grafton New Hall [193], a tentacular country house embedded in rolling English countryside.

By the end of the 1990s, reflecting the global reaction against unfettered capitalism, some architects had begun to turn against the new signature Modernism, looking for something more rooted in place. For example, the National Dance Centre in Edinburgh of 1999–2001 by Malcolm Fraser imaginatively wove together a miscellany of backland buildings and spaces on a steeply sloping site in the shadow of the Castle, while avoiding any flamboyant external gestures. And Page & Park, in designing a new Museum of Scottish Country Life in the countryside just outside Glasgow (1998–2001) [192], eschewed the flamboyant Supermodernism of the Museum of Scotland in favour of an emphatically sober, practical design. Its monumental, harled exterior and spatially complex internal disposition were designed to reflect the 18th- and 19th-century Improvement traditions of steading design.

The challenges of the new century of globalization were highlighted in the controversial project for a new Scottish Parliament at Holyrood, initiated in 1998. In a competition characterized by domineering monumental structures, the eventual winner seemed to be strikingly different. In keeping with his approach of organic deconstructivism, the Catalan architect Enric Miralles (1955–2000) envisaged an anti-monumental design dominated by natural shapes: the aim was merely 'to carve in the land . . . a gathering place'. His initial concept envisaged a scattering of shell-like structures, with roofs shaped like leaves or upturned boats [194]. In this apparently anarchic context, the only way left of communicating architectural meaning and status was through metaphoric, poetic motifs. Miralles's disavowal of traditional monumental grandeur was accentuated by the avant-garde, manifesto-like style of his presentations. But it was unclear whether his own design was any less rhetorical and image-driven than traditional classicism or Modernism – especially as, after his death, the design as executed by RMJM proved more dense and, in a word, monumental.

This loss of certainty in the architecture of ruling authority formed only one facet of a more general architectural dilemma. Internationally, no ethos or approach could any longer command general credibility. And for Scotland, it was a paradox that, alongside the proud talk of a national rebirth and of the central role to be played by architecture in 'building a nation', what was actually happening was a general international homogenization. Thus our story ends on an uncertain rather than triumphal note. As the new millennium dawned, the power of the market seemed to be fast swallowing up all the old, stimulating polarities and reference-points of architecture – the artistic and the rationalistic, the utopian and the pragmatic, the public and the private, the new and the old, and even the national and the universal – and what could replace them was by no means clear.

194 Scottish Parliament, Holyrood, Edinburgh, by Enric Miralles Benedetta Tagliabue (EMBT), 1999–2004: placard of collaged images and slogans prepared for the 1998 designer competition.

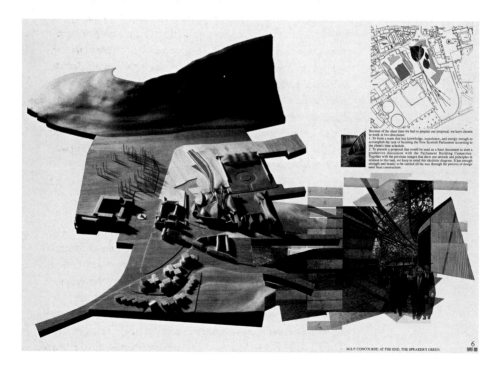

Conclusion

Can we, finally, isolate any common themes that draw together the centuries, even millennia, spanned by our story? We have to begin cautiously, as most definitions of 'national identity' are highly subjective constructions defined as much by the perceptions of others as by any innate essence, and this subjectivity is compounded when a series of these definitions is strung together into a 'tradition'. Common sense tells us that there can be no direct cultural or spiritual link, for example, between the builders of chambered tombs and the architects of today. This point is only underlined by the many past attempts to construct or evoke 'national tradition', all hopelessly beset by conflicting definitions.

Yet although there is clearly no such thing as a single 'grand tradition' of Scottish architecture, it would be equally misleading to see the latter as nothing more than a sequence of unrelated episodes. For a start, the geology and the equable, wet climate have remained reasonably unchanged. The most consistent thread in Scottish architecture has been the persistent use of stone construction, right through from the earliest times to the present day. But building in stone has not been continuous or exclusive, a fact often disguised by patterns of survival: turf or wooden buildings were ubiquitous for everyday purposes right up until the 19th century, while in the prehistoric era the archaeological evidence is skewed towards Orkney and other areas rich in massive stone monuments. Nor has it been consistent: methods have varied from the massive harled rubble of medieval castles and the ashlar of medieval churches to the composite stone-iron-wood construction of the 19th century city and the thin stone cladding of today.

By careful comparison with other countries, various subordinate themes also emerge within our story, especially in recent centuries. Perhaps the most obvious case is the prestige of

195 Composite painting showing the principal works of R. A. Lawson, a Scottish-born architect who designed many of the most important early buildings of the city of Dunedin, Otago Settlement, New Zealand. In this detail of the painting by George O'Brien, c. 1870, the central spire is that of the First Presbyterian Church. Otago was founded in 1848 (eight years after British annexation of New Zealand) by Free Church colonists from Scotland. In this ambiguous cultural context, colonial as well as 'Scottish', Lawson's designs mostly avoid specifically 'Scottish' styles, other than an occasional crowstepped gable or crown steeple.

the Scottish castle as building type and image, right through from the 14th to the 17th century and on, in consciously revived form, into the 19th century. The reasons for its popularity have been hotly disputed: while R. W. Billings in the 1840s assumed it was the unintentionally picturesque by-product of barons who 'cared for nothing but eating, drinking and fighting', barely fifty years later Robert Lorimer, like today's historians, could see the castle above all as 'a Scotch gentleman's home'. But whatever the rhetoric and the theories, its pervasiveness and persistence on the ground cannot be denied. Equally, one could point to the special strength of classical architecture, in all its variety, from the 16th to the 20th century, especially in contrast to the special veneration for Gothic in England, and the bolder embrace of Modernist avant-gardism on the Continent. Or there was the more generally high status of secular as against religious architecture, even before the Reformation.

But paradoxically, the most important 'tradition' of all, especially in the more recent time from the 16th century onwards, has been the constant eager embrace of radical change and discontinuity – to a degree unmatched by any other small country. Scotland had hardly completed its revolutionary purge of the trappings of conventional religious architecture when its union with England, and its welcome as a full partner in the empire, opened up a succession of even more dramatic ruptures in the built environment. Improvement, urbanization, industrial growth: each was matched by an ever bolder architectural diversity, until the climax was reached in the fearsomely vigorous architectural culture of Thomson, Burnet, Geddes and Mackintosh.

That individualistic world was torn down by the planned social reconstructions of the 20th-century years of retrenchment. Only now, in the new era of home rule, is there a renewed desire to express 'national pride' in building – against the unpromising backdrop of rampant global capitalism. Traditionally, the architectural rhetoric of national identity and myth-making has tended to vilify the 19th century in favour of a pre-industrial, or even pre-Union, golden age. But if this account has shown anything, the reverse is true: if there ever was a golden age of Scottish architecture, it was the Victorian era of imperialism and British global might. The challenge now is whether that achievement can be matched again by future generations of Scots, without the supporting infrastructure of empire and world economic dominance.

Bibliography

abbreviations
JSAH Journal of the Society of Architectural Historians
PSAS Proceedings of the Society of Antiquaries of Scotland
RCAHMS Royal Commission on the Ancient and Historical Monuments of Scotland
RIAS Royal Incorporation of Architects in Scotland
SAS Society of Antiquaries of Scotland

General Accounts

For a detailed textbook treatment of the post-Renaissance years (corresponding roughly to Chapters 3–6 of this book), together with a 'dictionary of architects', readers should consult our earlier book, A History of Scottish Architecture from the Renaissance to the Present Day (1996). Other significant books spanning several of the chapter periods of this volume include:

Breeze, D. (ed.) Studies in Scottish Antiquity, 1984
Cameron, N. de S. (ed.) Dictionary of Scottish Church History, 1993
Colvin, H. A Biographical Dictionary of British Architects 1660–1840, 1978 edn
—— and J. Harris (eds) The Country Seat, 1970
Cowan, E. J., and R. A. McDonald Alba, 2000
Devine, T. The Scottish Nation, 1700–2000, 1999
Drummond, A. L. The Church Architecture of Protestantism, 1934
Dunbar, J. G. The Architecture of Scotland, 1978 edn
Glendinning, M., A. MacKechnie and R. Oram The Architecture of Sovereignty, 2003
Gordon, G. (ed.) Perspectives of the Scottish City, 1985
Gow, I. R., and A. Rowan (eds) The Scottish Country House, 1995
Henderson, G. and I. The Art of the Picts, 2004
Houston, R. A., and W. W. J. Knox (eds) The New Penguin History of Scotland, 2001
Kidd, C. 'The Canon of Patriotic Landmarks in Scottish History', Scotlands, 1, 1994
Lynch, M. (ed.) The Oxford Companion to Scottish History, 2001
Macdonald, M. Scottish Art, 2000
Macmillan Encyclopedia of Architects, 1982
Mays, D. (ed.) The Architecture of Scottish Cities, 1997
National Library of Scotland, Edinburgh Scottish Architects at Home and Abroad, 1978
Stell, G., J. Shaw and S. Storrier Scottish Life and Society: Scotland's Buildings, 2002
Warrack, J. Domestic Life in Scotland, 1488–1688, 1920

Chapter 1

Adams, D. Brechin Round Tower: an Illustrated Guide, n.d.
Alcock, L., et al. 'Reconnaissance excavations on Early Historic sites', PSAS, 116, 1986, 255–79
Alcock, L., and E. A. Alcock 'Reconnaissance excavations on early historic fortifications', PSAS, 122, 1992, 215–87
—— 'The Context of the Dupplin Cross', PSAS, 126, 1996, 455–57

Armit, I. The Archaeology of Skye and the Western Isles, 1996
—— Celtic Scotland, 1997
—— Scotland's Hidden History, 1998
—— Towers in the North – the Brochs of Scotland, 2003
—— and N. Fojut Dun Charlabhaigh and the Hebridean Iron Age, 1998
Ascherson, J. A., I. Banks and J. O'Sullivan (eds) Nationalism and Archaeology, 1996
Ashmore, P. Calanais: the Standing Stones, 1995
—— Neolithic and Bronze Age Scotland, 1996
Barclay, A., and J. Harding (eds) Pathways and Ceremonies: the Cursus Monuments of Britain and Ireland (Neolithic Studies Group Seminar Papers, 4), 1999
Barclay, G. Balfarg: the Prehistoric Ceremonial Complex, n.d.
—— (ed.) The Making of Scotland, 1998
—— and G. Maxwell The Cleaven Dyke and Littleour (SAS monograph 13), 1998
——, K. Brophy and G. MacGregor 'A Neolithic building at Claish Farm', Antiquity, 76, 2002, 23–24
Bidwell, P. Roman Forts in Britain, 1997
Bradley, R. Altering the Earth (SAS Monograph 8), 1993
Breeze, D. Ardoch, the Roman Fort, 1998
—— Roman Scotland, 1996
Broun, D., and T. Clancy (eds) Spes Scottorum: the Hope of Scots, 1999
Cameron, N. M. 'St Rule's Church, St Andrews', PSAS, 124, 1994, 367–78
Campbell, E. Saints and Sea-Kings, 1999
Fairweather, A., and I. Ralston 'The Neolithic timber hall at Balbridie', Antiquity, 67, 1993, 313–23
Fernie, E. 'Early church architecture in Scotland', PSAS, 116, 1986, 393–411
Fisher, I. Early Medieval Sculpture in the West Highlands and Islands, 2001
Fojut, N. 'Is Mousa a broch?', PSAS, 11, 1981, 220–28
Foster, S. Picts, Gaels and Scots, 1996
—— (ed.) Scottish Power Centres, 1998
—— (ed.) The St Andrews Sarcophagus, 1998
—— Place, Space and Odyssey, 2001
Grant, A., and K. Stringer Medieval Scotland, 1993
Hanson, W. S., and E. A. Slater (eds) Scottish Archaeology: New Perceptions, 1991, 81–111
Harbison, P. Irish Church Crosses, 1994
Henshall, A. S., and J. N. G. Ritchie The Chambered Cairns of the Central Highlands, 2001
Hingley, R. 'Society in Scotland from 700 BC to AD 200', PSAS, 22, 1992, 7–53
Jervise, A. 'Remarks on the Round Tower of Brechin', PSAS, ii, 1857–60, 28–35
Lang, J. T. 'Hogback monuments of Scotland', PSAS, 105, 1975, 207
MacKie, E. W. The Roundhouses, Brochs and Wheelhouses of Atlantic Scotland, pt 1, 2002
Mann, J. C. 'The construction of the Antonine Wall', PSAS, 116, 1986, 191–93
Martlew, R. 'The typological study of the structures of brochs', PSAS, 112, 1982, 254–76
Mithen, S. (ed.) Hunter-Gatherer Landscape Archaeology, 2 vols, 2000
Morrison, I. Landscape with Lake Dwellings, 1985
Phillips, T. Landscapes of the Living, Landscapes of the Dead, 2002
Pitts, L., and J. K. St Joseph Inchtuthil: the Roman Legionary Fortress (Britannia Monograph Series, 5), 1985

RCAHMS Argyll: An Inventory of the Monuments, 4, Iona, 1982
Rideout, J., et al. Hillforts of Southern Scotland, 1992
Ritchie, A. Viking Scotland, 1993
—— Iona, 1997
—— (ed.) Neolithic Orkney in its European Context, 2000
Ritchie, J. N. G. Brochs of Scotland, 1998
Royal Archaeological Institute The St Andrews Area, 1991
Smith, B. B., and I. Banks In the Shadow of the Brochs – the Iron Age in Scotland, 2002
Stalley, R. Early Medieval Architecture, 1999
Veitch, K. 'The Columban Church in Northern Britain', PSAS, 127, 1997, 627–47
Wickham-Jones, C. R. Scotland's First Settlers, 1994
Woolliscroft, D. J. The Roman Frontier on the Gask Ridge, 2002

Chapter 2

Billings, R. W. The Baronial and Ecclesiastical Antiquities of Scotland, 4 vols, 1845–52
Caldwell, D., and G. Ewart 'Finlaggan and the Lordship of the Isles', Scottish Historical Review, Oct. 1993, 146–66
Campbell, I. 'A Romanesque Revival and the Early Renaissance in Scotland', JSAH, Sept. 1995
Coldstream, N. Medieval Architecture, 2002
Cruden, S. The Scottish Castle, 1963
Dennison, E. P., D. Ditchburn and M. Lynch (eds) Aberdeen before 1800: A New History, 2002
Dunbar, J. G. Scottish Royal Palaces, 1999
—— 'The medieval architecture of the Scottish Highlands', in L. MacLean (ed.), The Middle Ages in the Highlands, 1981
Fawcett, R. Edinburgh Castle, 1986
—— The Abbey and Palace of Dunfermline, 1990
—— The Castles of Fife, 1993
—— Scottish Architecture from the accession of the Stewarts to the Reformation, 1994
—— Scottish Medieval Churches, 2002
Fenton, S., and G. Stell (eds) Loads and Roads in Scotland and Beyond, 1984
Ferguson, J. Linlithgow Palace, 1901
Foster, S. (ed.) Scottish Power Centres, 1998
Grant, A., and K. Stringer Medieval Scotland, 1993
Liszka, T. R., and L. E. M. Walker (eds) The North Sea World in the Middle Ages, 2001
Lynch, M., M. Spearman and G. Stell (eds) The Scottish Medieval Town, 1988
MacGibbon, D., and T. Ross The Castellated and Domestic Architecture of Scotland, 5 vols, 1887–92
—— The Ecclesiastical Architecture of Scotland, 3 vols, 1896–97
MacIvor, I. A Fortified Frontier, 2001
McRoberts D. (ed.) The Medieval Church of St Andrews, 1976
Newton, N., and E. Talbot 'Excavations at the Peel of Lumphanan', PSAS, 128, 1998, 653–70
Oram, R. The Kings and Queens of Scotland, 2001
Royal Archaeological Institute The St Andrews Area, 1991
Simpson, A. T., and S. Stevenson (eds) Town Houses and Structures in Medieval Scotland, 1980
Stalley, R. Early Medieval Architecture, 1999
Steer, K. A., and J. Bannerman Late Medieval Monumental Sculpture in the West Highlands, 1977

Stell, G. 'Architecture: the changing needs of society', in J. Brown (ed.), *Scottish Society in the Fifteenth Century*, 1977
—— *Dunstaffnage and the Castles of Argyll*, 1994
Sweetman, D. *The Origin and Development of the Tower-House*, 2000
Tabraham, C. 'The Scottish medieval towerhouse as lordly residence', *PSAS*, 118, 1988, 267–76
Thurlby, M. 'Aspects of the architectural history of Kirkwall Cathedral', *PSAS*, 127, 1997, 855–88
Williams, J. H. (ed.) *Stewart Style*, 1996
Yeoman, P. *Medieval Scotland*, 1995
Zeune, J. *The Last Scottish Castles*, 1992

Chapter 3
Apted, M. R. *Painted Ceilings of Scotland*, 1966
Bath, M. 'Alexander Seton's Painted Gallery', in L. Gent (ed.), *Albion's Classicism*, 1995
Billings, R. W. *The Baronial and Ecclesiastical Antiquities of Scotland*, 4 vols, 1845–52
Cavers, K. *A Vision of Scotland: The Nation observed by John Slezer*, 1993
Colvin, H. 'A Scottish Origin for English Palladianism?', *Architectural History*, 17, 1974
—— 'The Beginnings of the Architectural Profession in Scotland', *Architectural History*, 29, 1986
Cunningham, I. C. (ed.) *The Nation Survey'd*, 2001
Dennison, E. P., D. Ditchburn and M. Lynch (eds) *Aberdeen before 1800: A New History*, 2002
Goodare, J., and M. Lynch *The Reign of James VI*, 2000
Hannay, R. K., and C. P. H. Watson 'The Building of the Parliament House', *Book of the Old Edinburgh Club*, 13, 1924
Howard, D. *Scottish Architecture, Reformation to Restoration*, 1995
Imrie, J., and J. G. Dunbar *Accounts of the Masters of Works*, 2, 1982
Louw, H. J. 'The Origin of the Sash-window', *Architectural History*, 26, 1983
Lowrey, J. 'A Man of Excellent Parts', 1987
Macaulay, J. *The Classical Country House in Scotland*, 1987
MacGibbon, D., and T. Ross *The Castellated and Domestic Architecture of Scotland*, 5 vols, 1887–92
—— *The Ecclesiastical Architecture of Scotland*, 3 vols, 1896–97
MacIvor, I. *A Fortified Frontier*, 2001
McKean, C. *The Scottish Chateau*, 2001
MacKechnie, A. 'Scots Court Architecture of the early 17th century' (PhD thesis, University of Edinburgh, 1993)
Mylne, R. S. *The Master Masons to the Crown of Scotland*, 1893
—— 'The Masters of Work to the Crown of Scotland', *PSAS*, 30, 1896
Paton, H. M. (ed.) *Accounts of the Masters of Works*, 1, 1957
Royal Archaeological Institute *The St Andrews Area*, 1991
Scottish Arts Council *Sir William Bruce*, 1970 (intro. by J. G. Dunbar)
James Smith Anniversary Committee *Minerva's Flame*, 1995
Society of Architectural Historians of Great Britain *Classicism in Scotland 1670–1748* (1983 conference papers)
Stell, G. P. 'The earliest Tolbooths', *PSAS*, 1981

Chapter 4
Adam, R. *Ruins of the Palace of Spalatro, in Dalmatia*, 1764
—— and J. Adam *Works in Architecture of Robert and James Adam*, 3 vols, 1773–1822 (vol. 1, 5 parts, issued 1773–78; vol. 2, 1779; vol. 3, 1822; all reissued, ed. R. Oresko, 1975)
Adam, W. *Vitruvius Scoticus*, 1812 (reprint, ed. J. Simpson, 1980)
Allan, D. *Scotland in the 18th Century*, 2001
Beard, G. *The Work of Robert Adam*, 1978
Bolton, A. *The Architecture of Robert and James Adam*, 2 vols, 1922
Brogden, W. A. (ed.) *The Neo-Classical Town*, 1996
Campbell, C., et al., *Vitruvius Britannicus*, 3 vols, 1715–25
Colley, L. *Britons*, 1993
Donnachie, I., and G. Hewitt *Historic New Lanark*, 1993
Fleming, J. *Robert Adam and his Circle*, 1962
Frew, J., and D. Jones (eds) *Aspects of Scottish Classicism*, 1989
Friedman, T. *James Gibbs*, 1984
Gifford, J. *William Adam*, 1989
Goodfellow, G. 'Colen Campbell's Shawfield Mansion', *JSAH*, 23, 1964
Gow, I. R. *The Edinburgh Villa* (BA thesis, Cambridge University), 1975
Harris, E. *The Genius of Robert Adam – his Interiors*, 2001
Harris, J. *Sir William Chambers*, 1970
Hay, G. *The Architecture of Scottish Post-Reformation Churches*, 1957
Holloway, J. *The Norie Family*, 1994
King, D. *The Complete Works of Robert and James Adam*, 1991
Kinnear, H. 'John Douglas's Country House Designs', *Architectural Heritage*, xii, 2001, 1–12
Lindsay, I. G. *Georgian Edinburgh*, 1948
—— and M. Cosh *Inveraray and the Dukes of Argyll*, 1973
Macaulay, J. *The Gothic Revival 1745–1845*, 1975
—— *The Classical Country House in Scotland*, 1987
Markus, T. A. (ed.) *Order in Space and Society*, 1982
—— *Buildings and Power*, 1993
Moss, M. *The 'Magnificent Castle' of Culzean*, 2002
Philipson, N. T., and R. Mitchison (eds) *Scotland in the Age of Improvement*, 1970
Pryke, S. 'Hopetoun House', *Country Life*, 10 Aug. 1995
Rae, I. *Charles Cameron*, 1971
Rowan, A. 'The Building of Hopetoun', *Architectural History*, 27 1984
—— *Catalogue of Architectural Drawings in the Victoria and Albert Museum: Robert Adam*, 1988
—— 'Bob the Roman': Heroic Antiquity and the Architecture of Robert Adam (exh. cat., Sir John Soane's Museum, London), 2003
Sanderson, M. H. B. *Robert Adam and Scotland*, 1992
Shvidkovsky, D. *The Empress and the Architect* [on Charles Cameron], 1996
Stevenson, C. *Medicine and Magnificence: British Hospital and Asylum Architecture, 1660–1815*, 2000
Stewart, M. C. H. *Lord Mar's Plans, 1700–32* (M.Litt. thesis, University of Glasgow), 1988
—— 'The Earl of Mar and Scottish Baroque', *Architectural Heritage*, ix, 1998, 16–30

Stutchbury, H. E. *The Architecture of Colen Campbell*, 1967
Tait, A. A. *The Landscape Garden in Scotland*, 1980
—— *Robert Adam: Drawings and Imagination*, 1993
Youngson, A. J. *The Making of Classical Edinburgh*, 1975

Chapter 5
Aberdeen Civic Society *Archibald Simpson*, 1978
Allen, N. (ed.) *Scottish Pioneers of the Greek Revival*, 1984
Billings, R. W. *The Baronial and Ecclesiastical Antiquities of Scotland*, 4 vols, 1845–52
Bonnar, T. *Biographical Sketch of George Meikle Kemp*, 1892
Gordon Bowe, N., and E. Cumming *The Arts and Crafts Movement in Dublin and Edinburgh*, 1998
Brogden, W. A. (ed.) *The Neo-Classical Town*, 1996
Brown, S. J., and M. Fry (eds), *Scotland in the Age of the Disruption*, 1993
Cruft, K., and A. Fraser (eds) *James Craig*, 1995
Cumming, E. S. *Arts and Crafts in Edinburgh*, 1985
—— *Phoebe Anna Traquair*, 1993
——, and W. Caplan *The Arts and Crafts Movement*, 1991
Dixon, R., and S. Muthesius *Victorian Architecture*, 1978
Donnelly, M. *Scotland's Stained Glass*, 1997
Edwards, B. 'The Glasgow Improvement Scheme', *Planning History*, 12:3, 1990
Fenton, A., and B. Walker *The Rural Architecture of Scotland*, 1981
Fiddes, V., and A. Rowan *David Bryce*, 1976
Fraser, W. H., and C. H. Lee (eds) *Aberdeen 1800–2000: A New History*, 2000
Frew, J., and D. Jones (eds) *The New Town Phenomenon: The Second Generation*, 2000
—— *Scotland and Europe*, 1991
Gomme, A., and D. M. Walker *Architecture of Glasgow*, 1968
Gow, I. R. *William Henry Playfair* (RIAS exhibition text), 1988.
—— *The Scottish Interior*, 1992
—— and T. Clifford *The National Gallery of Scotland*, 1988
Hardie, E. *A Short History of ... Scott Morton and Tynecastle Co.*, 1976
Home, R. *Of Planting and Planning*, 1997
Hunter Blair, D. *John Patrick, Third Marquess of Bute*, 1921
Jeffery, T. M. *The Life and Works of F.T. Pilkington* (B.Arch. thesis, Newcastle University), 1976
Kinchin, P. and J. *Glasgow's Great Exhibitions*, 1988
McAra, D. *Sir James Gowans*, 1975
Macaulay, J. *The Gothic Revival 1745–1845*, 1975
—— 'The Architectural Collaboration between J. Gillespie Graham and A. W. N. Pugin', *Architectural History*, 27, 1984
—— *The Classical Country House in Scotland*, 1987
McFadzean, R. *The Life and Work of Alexander Thomson*, 1979
Mackechnie, A. (ed.) *David Hamilton, Architect*, 1993
McKinstry, S. *Rowand Anderson*, 1991
Markus, T. A. (ed.) *Order in Space and Society*, 1982
—— *Buildings and Power*, 1993
Maver, I. *Glasgow*, 2001

Maxwell Scott, W. *Abbotsford*, 1982

Nicoll, J. (ed.), *Domestic Architecture in Scotland*, 1908

Reed, P. *Glasgow: The Forming of a City*, 1993

Rock, J. *Thomas Hamilton, Architect*, 1984

Royal Institute of British Architects *James MacLaren*, 1990

Ruskin, J. *Lectures on Architecture and Painting* delivered at Edinburgh, 1854

Savage, P. *Lorimer and the Edinburgh Craft Designers*, 1980

Scottish Vernacular Buildings Working Group *Highland Vernacular Building*, 1989

Sinclair, F. (ed.) *Charles Wilson Architect*, 1995

Smailes, H. *A Portrait Gallery for Scotland*, 1985

Stamp, G. (ed.) *The Light of Truth and Beauty: The Lectures of Alexander 'Greek' Thomson*, 1999

—— *Robert Weir Schultz*, 1981

—— and S. McKinstry (eds) *Greek Thomson*, 1994

Wainwright, C. *The Romantic Interior*, 1989

Walker, D. M. 'William Burn', in J. Fawcett (ed.), *Seven Victorian Architects*, 1976

—— 'The Rhind Lectures: a Synopsis', *PSAS*, 121, 1991

Young, W. *The Municipal Buildings, Glasgow*, 1890

Youngson, A. J. *The Making of Classical Edinburgh*, 1975

Chapter 6

Abercrombie, P., and D. Plumstead *A Civic Survey and Plan for Edinburgh*, 1949

—— and R. Matthew *The Clyde Valley Regional Plan 1946*, 1949

Architectural Design, May 1963 (special issue on Cumbernauld New Town)

Begg, T. *Fifty Special Years*, 1987

Benson & Forsyth, *The Museum of Scotland*, 1999

Black, D. *All the First Minister's Men*, 2001

Brett, D. *Charles Rennie Mackintosh*, 1992

Sir J. Burnet & Partners, *The Architectural Work of Sir J. Burnet & Partners*, 1930

Lord Bute, *A Plea for Scotland's Architectural Heritage*, 1936

Campbell, L. *Coventry Cathedral*, 1996

Chapman W. D. and C. F. Riley *Granite City*, 1952

Crampsey, R. *The Empire Exhibition of 1938*, 1988

Crawford, A. *Charles Rennie Mackintosh*, 1995

Edwards, B. *Basil Spence 1907–1976*, 1995

Fraser, W. H., and C. H. Lee (eds) *Aberdeen 1800–2000: A New History*, 2000

Frew, J. 'Towards a municipal housing blueprint', *Architectural Heritage*, xi, 2000

Corporation of Glasgow, *Municipal Glasgow*, 1914

[Glasgow Empire Exhibition] *Exhibition Official Guide*, 1938

Glendinning, M. (ed.) *The Rebuilding of Scotland*, 1997

——, A. MacKechnie and R. Oram *The Architecture of Sovereignty*, 2003

—— and S. Muthesius *Tower Block*, 1994

—— and D. Page *Clone City: Crisis and Renewal in Contemporary Scotish Architecture*, 1999

—— and D. Watters (eds) *Home Builders*, 1952

Howarth, T. *Charles Rennie Mackintosh and the Modern Movement*, 1952

Jury, A. G. *Glasgow's Housing Centenary*, 1966

Keating, M. *The Designation of Cumbernauld New Town*, 1986

Kelsall, M., and S. Harris *A Future for the Past*, 1961

Kinchin, P. and J. *Glasgow's Great Exhibitions*, 1988

Lowrey, J. (ed.) *The Age of Mackintosh* (*Architectural Heritage*, 3, 1992)

Macaulay, J. *Glasgow School of Art*, 1993

—— *Hill House*, 1994

Mac Journal One: Gillespie Kidd & Coia, 1994

MacDonald, S. (ed.) *Scottish Architecture 2000–2002*, 2002

McKean, C. *The Scottish Thirties*, 1987

—— *The Making of the Museum of Scotland*, 2000

McKean, J. *C. R. Mackintosh*, 2001

Macleod, R. *Charles Rennie Mackintosh*, 1968

Marks, R., R. Scott, B. Gasson, J. Thomson and P. Vainker *The Burrell Collection*, 1983

Matthew, R. H., J. Reid and M. Lindsay (eds) *The Conservation of Georgian Edinburgh*, 1972

Matthew, S. R. *The Knights and Chapel of the Thistle*, 1988

Mears, F. *A Regional Survey and Plan for Central and South-East Scotland*, 1949

Meller, H. *Patrick Geddes*, 1990

Muthesius, S. *The Postwar University*, 2000

Nuttgens, P. *Reginald Fairlie*, 1959

Payne, P. L. *The Hydro*, 1988

Purves, G. A. S. *An Introduction to the Work of Sir F. Mears*, 1983 (Heriot-Watt University, Edinburgh, Research Paper 4)

Reiach, A., and R. Hurd *Building Scotland*, 1941/1944

RIAS *Scottish Architecture in the Nineteen-Eighties*, 1987

Richards, J., *Sir Robert Matthew and his Work*, 1984 (lecture text)

Robertson, P. (ed.) *Charles Rennie Mackintosh – The Architectural Papers*, 1990

Rogerson, R. W. K. *Jack Coia*, 1986

Savage, P. *Lorimer and the Edinburgh Craft Designers*, 1980

Scott & Wilson, Kirkpatrick & Partners, *Report on a Highway Plan for Glasgow*, 1965

Scottish Housing Advisory Committee, *Planning Our New Homes* (Westwood Report), 1944

Scott-Moncrieff, G. *Living Traditions of Scotland*, 1951

Service, A. (ed.) *Edwardian Architecture and its Origins*, 1975

Sharp, D., and C. Cooke (eds) *The Modern Movement in Architecture*, 2000, 225–32

Sloan, A. *James Miller*, 1993

Walker, D. M. *St Andrew's House*, 1989

—— 'Listing in Scotland', *Transactions of the Ancient Monuments Society*, 38, 1994

Watters, D. M. *Cardross Seminary*, 1997

Weaver, L. *The Scottish National War Memorial*, 1927

Welter, V. *Biopolis: Patrick Geddes and the City of Life*, 2002

—— and J. Lawson (eds) *The City after Patrick Geddes*, 2000

Willis, P. *New Architecture in Scotland*, 1977

RCAHMS inventories

Argyll, 7 vols, 1971–92

Berwick, revised 1915

Caithness, 1911

Dumfries, 1920

East Lothian, 1924

[City of] Edinburgh, 1951

Fife, Kinross and Clackmannan, 1933

Kirkcudbright, 1914

Midlothian and West Lothian, 1929

Orkney, 1946

Outer Isles, 1928

Peebles, 1967

Roxburgh, 1956

Selkirk, 1957

Shetland, 1946

Stirlingshire, 2 vols, 1963

Sutherland, 1911

Wigtown, 1911

Buildings of Scotland series: volumes published to date

Argyll and Bute, by F. A. Walker, 2000

Dumfries and Galloway, by J. Gifford, 1996

Edinburgh, by J. Gifford, C. McWilliam and D. M. Walker, 1984

Fife, by J. Gifford, 1988

Glasgow, by E. Williamson, A. Riches and M. Higgs, 1990

Highland and Islands, by J. Gifford, 1992

Lothian (except Edinburgh), by C. McWilliam, 1978

Stirling and Central Scotland, by J. Gifford and F. A. Walker, 2002

Acknowledgments for Illustrations

Aberdeen Aerial Survey 34; Bedford Lemere 171; Cambridge University Council of Aerial Photography 9; Central Office of Information (Crown Copyright) 184, 186, 187; Dennis Coutts 189; Cumbernauld Development Corporation 179; Dundee Public Libraries 100; Edinburgh Central Library 17; Edinburgh University Library 101; Dr Richard Fawcett 37, 45–49; Collection: Glasgow School of Art 163; Miles Glendinning 71, 139, 159, 182, 183, 185; Guthrie Photography 155; Historic Scotland 2, 4, 14, 19–22, 29, 32, 38, 43, 50, 67, 106; Photo Angelo Hornak 169; © Hunterian Art Gallery, University of Glasgow, Mackintosh Collection, Glasgow (Photo Media Services, Glasgow University) 165; © Emily Lane 59, 63, 66, 79, 87, 88, 117, 168, 172; National Galleries of Scotland 81, 114; Photos Anthony Kersting 89, 90, 99; National Museums of Scotland 16, 191; Otago Settlers Museum, Dunedin, New Zealand 195; Page & Park 192; Perth Art Gallery 129; Planair 180; RCAHMS (Crown Copyright) 3, 5–8, 11–13, 15, 18, 23–28, 30, 33, 35, 36, 41, 42, 44, 51, 52, 54–58, 60–62, 64, 70, 73–78, 83–85, 91–94, 96–98, 104, 107–12, 115, 116, 119–21, 123, 124, 126–128, 130–35, 137, 138, 141–48, 151, 153, 154, 156, 157, 160–62, 164, 166, 170, 173, 175–77, 188; RMJM 181, 194; Roman Michnowicz 1, 190; Royal Incorporation of Architects in Scotland 68, 69, 113, 122, 142, 150, 158; Edwin Smith 53; Sir John Soane's Museum, London 105; Society for the Promotion of Roman Studies 10; Photo Laurie Strachan 174; Studio Brett, Glasgow 178; Ushida Findlay 193. Ill. 65 is from D. MacGibbon and T. Ross, *The Castellated and Domestic Architecture of Scotland*, 1, 1887.

Index

Figures in *italic* type indicate pages on which illustrations appear